# SUPER TEAM

## THE WARRIORS' QUEST FOR THE NEXT NBA DYNASTY

BayArea
NewsGroup

T0155207

(Jane Tyska/Staff)

(Nhat V. Meyer/Staff)

This book is available in quantity at special discounts for your group or organization. For further information, contact:

**Triumph Books LLC**
814 North Franklin Street
Chicago, Illinois 60610
Phone: (312) 337-0747
www.triumphbooks.com

Printed in U.S.A.
Hardcover ISBN: 978-1-62937-443-7
Paperback ISBN: 978-1-62937-415-4

**Bay Area News Group**
Sharon Ryan, Publisher and President
Neil Chase, Executive Editor
Bert Robinson, Managing Editor
Bud Geracie, Executive Sports Editor

Interior Design: Patricia Frey
Cover Design: Andy Hansen

Front cover photos by Aric Crabb/Staff (Durant and Curry), Nhat V. Meyer/Staff (Thompson and Green) and Jose Carlos Fajardo/Staff (Kerr). Back cover photo by Aric Crabb/Staff.

(Nhat V. Meyer/Staff)

# CONTENTS

# INTRODUCTION

## By Marcus Thompson II

Stephen Curry was in a college gym, working with the best young players in the area at a clinic sponsored by Under Armour. Outside, thousands of fans had gathered, swarming the perimeter of the gym, trying to get a glimpse of the Warriors' superstar.

When Curry finally went outside to salute the crowd, he found thousands of people serenading him with screams, many of them wearing his No. 30 jersey.

This happened 7,000 miles away from the Bay Area. At Guangzhou University. In China.

The No. 30 is now etched in Golden State lore. It is a symbol of Warriors elitism. It is the logo of a once-in-a-generation player who has orchestrated this era of Bay Area hoop dominance. It is something that declares such greatness that in some quarters it is seen as arrogance.

This is all so surreal.

An elite franchise? Golden State with a player for the ages? Warriors and arrogance in the same sentence?

Looking at the Warriors now, most see a championship contender, a super team loaded with All-Stars and future Hall of Famers. With Curry, Klay Thompson, Draymond Green and Kevin Durant, the Warriors are NBA gluttons. Basketball's one-percenters.

Such an existence never seemed possible for the Warriors. Such heights weren't visible from the depths where the Warriors' dwelled. Those who followed the Warriors through any significant portion of their 40 years in the wilderness are still grappling with this new reality.

That includes Warriors G.M. Bob Myers. He grew up in the Bay Area. He grew up a Warriors fan.

"If you're a fan of this team, you had to be patient," Myers said recently. "You had to wait. And I feel like for our fans, they deserve to watch a team like this. Our fans are the best. They stuck with some tough stuff to watch."

To see how crazy it is to find the Warriors in their current state, just follow the No. 30 jersey through franchise history.

Steph Curry has sparked a Warriors renaissance and brought new meaning to the No. 30 he wears. (Jose Carlos Fajardo/Staff)

Darnell Hillman was the first Warrior to wear it, in 1979, and its future already was being foretold.

Hillman had been the Warriors No. 1 pick in 1971, No. 8 overall. But he opted for the ABA. The Indiana Pacers offered him more money and the Warriors didn't match.

The leagues merged in 1976, bringing Hillman to the NBA. He didn't sign with the Warriors until 20-plus games into the 1979-80 season. It turned out to be his final season, and the fourth consecutive season of declining fortunes for the Warriors.

The Warriors had followed their championship in 1975 with a 59-win season in 1976. But then the victory total dropped to 46, then 43, then 38, then 24.

But then along came Bernard King, the next No. 30.

At 6-foot-7, King was an elite talent, a scoring phenom. But he was a troubled soul, turning up on police blotters while in college at Tennessee and in the pros with the New York Nets and Utah Jazz. That's how the Warriors got him in 1980, for cheap: all it took was back-up big man Wayne Cooper and a second-round pick.

King not only stayed out of trouble with the Warriors, he looked every bit the franchise centerpiece. He averaged 21.9 points on 58.8 percent shooting, with 6.8 rebounds, as the Warriors improved by 15 wins. King was named NBA Comeback Player of the Year.

The next season, King was even better: 23.2 points and his first All-Star bid.

King, a resurrected star, took a bigger offer from the New York Knicks. He became a Hall of Famer for them.

Jersey No. 30 embodied how this franchise didn't deserve such rich talent.

Cash-strapped and living in the shadow of the Lakers, the Warriors were becoming an operation that couldn't keep its stars. They were unworthy of the league's best.

Golden State faithfuls can run off the long list of superstars who went away, players who looked capable of taking the Warriors to new levels but wound up with more legitimate franchises. Being a Warriors fan meant watching your star go shine elsewhere. Rick Barry. Jamaal Wilkes. Robert Parish. Bernard King.

Mitch Richmond was a legit scorer the day he stepped on an NBA court. The Warriors drafted him No. 5 overall out of Kansas State in 1988. He averaged 22 points his rookie season. The next season, he was part of a legendary trio of with Chris Mullin and Tim Hardaway.

The Warriors were a hot upstart. They twice pulled off first-round upsets. Run TMC, as the trio was known, was the highest scoring trio in the NBA. The Warriors were relevant in the NBA even though not a legitimate contender. Their style of play, fast-paced and high-scoring, was an exciting contribution to the NBA landscape. The Warriors were electrifying.

And then the Warriors traded Richmond. Don Nelson, the mastermind of Warriors' basketball, was looking to take his scheme to a new level. Unable to land the dominant big man that dictated the balance of power in the league, Nelson opted for a "small ball approach."

His ideal scenario was five players on the court with guard-like skills who can run. He wanted to combat size with quickness, offset power with skill.

This style of play made Billy Owens looks incredibly appealing to Nelson. A star at

Syracuse, Owens was a 6-foot-8 forward who could handle the ball and pass like a guard. He had enough size to force opponents to put a big man on him and enough skill tò draw those big men out of the paint.

Owens wore No. 30. In three seasons with the Warriors, he averaged 15 points on 51.2 percent shooting with 7.9 rebounds and 3.4 assists. But he wasn't a game changer. He wasn't the difference-maker that made it worth losing Richmond, who went on to become a Hall of Famer.

Owens never lived up the expectations of the trade. He was eventually traded to Miami. And No. 30 became a marker of disappointment. It represented the futility of Warriors' management, swapping great for good, letting gems slip through their fingers.

Which is why it is fitting that John Starks wore No. 30 for the Warriors.

He made his NBA debut with Golden State in 1988-89. He had a lot of growing to do — he was raw talent with immaturity issues — but was clearly talented. He just wasted away

The trade for Billy Owens (above) broke up Run TMC by sending future Hall of Famer Mitch Richmond to Sacramento, and kept the franchise mired in mediocrity. (Gary Reyes/Staff)

Bernard King wore No. 30 in terrific fashion for the Warriors from 1980-1982 but left to spend the prime of his Hall of Fame career with the New York Knicks. (AP Images)

on the end of the Warriors bench until he was eventually cut.

Starks got away from the Warriors and landed with the Knicks, who developed his talent and honed him into a quality player. He was named All-NBA Defense second team in 1993, then registered an iconic dunk over Horace Grant and Michael Jordan in the playoffs. He became an All-Star in 1994. He won NBA Sixth Man of the Year in 1997.

Starks is a celebrated Knicks figures, a key player in one of the more memorable eras for the franchise. He came along way from lowly No. 30 on the Warriors, who couldn't make a diamond from his rough.

Warriors fans know this feeling too well. Bad trades, worse draft choices, suspect player development, brilliant ideas unraveling into two steps back instead of a step forward. Before stockpiling the best players in the league, the Warriors seemed to figure out new ways to lose them.

After Owens, the Warriors missed the playoffs for 12 straight seasons. And jersey No. 30 became the number of insignificance. It was suitable for 10-day contract players, journeymen making pit stops and busts hanging on in the league. Ben McDonald. Carl Thomas. Clarence Weatherspoon. Jamel Thomas. Bill Curley.

The Warriors were irrelevant, doormats. They went multiple generations without being viable contenders. They were so inept, making the playoffs became worthy of celebration. The teams that reached the second round became legends.

For so long, this was the Warriors' existence. Laughingstocks. A cursed franchise beleaguered by debilitating injuries and bad decisions.

And then along came Curry.

There were so many ways this could have gone another way, would have gone another way most times in Warriors history.

The Minnesota Timberwolves could have taken him in the 2009 draft; they need a point guard and had two picks before the Warriors at No. 9.

The Warriors could have traded their pick to Phoenix; it was all set up with Amar'e Stoudemire coming to Golden State in a deal that would now rival those that sent Chamberlain, Parrish, McHale, and Richmond elsewhere.

The Warriors could have acceded to the wishes of Curry's camp, which repeatedly begged the Warriors not to draft him.

But the Timberwolves picked two other point guards. And Warriors general manager Larry Riley ignored the pleas of Curry's camp to let him go to New York. And the Warriors nixed the trade arrangement they with Phoenix. All of the usual pratfalls were avoided.

Even when serious and chronic ankle sprains cast his career in doubt, Curry overcame them and avoided joining the long list of Warriors injury casualties.

Now, jersey No. 30, not worn from 2001 to 2009, represents a reversal of fortune. And the results are unfathomable to those who were around in the bad old days. 🏀

# FULL-COURT PRESS

## Media Coverage Intense on Curry, Durant & Co.

By Daniel Brown | September 27, 2016

There was no actual basketball played at Warriors media day. The only shots taken came from the clicking cameras documenting Kevin Durant's every long-legged step.

And so it began. The great NBA chemistry experiment is underway. Having fallen one game short of back-to-back titles, the Warriors responded by signing Durant, the biggest star on the market, and unleashing this: the biggest media day in Bay Area memory.

"I wouldn't say it's strange. It's new and fresh," Durant said. "I'm looking forward to it. I just got super excited as I was walking in here."

Durant wasn't the only one revved up. The Warriors issued a record number of press credentials this year, cutting things off at about 225 because there was no room left on the floor.

The usual alphabet soup of sports outlets were here — ESPN, TNT, NBA TV — but also CNBC, covering things from a technology angle. Several international outlets were on hand, meaning that Draymond Green quotes were being translated back to China, Turkey, France, Japan and Italy.

On one hand, there was a wide-array of questions ranging from the meaning of a Rick James tattoo (that one was for Durant) to attendance at yoga classes (Zaza Pachulia) to plans for the national anthem (every player).

But at the heart of it there was just one question: How will the Warriors bounce back from their epic collapse against the Cleveland Cavaliers in the NBA Finals?

Kevin Durant speaks with the big media contingent during practice. The media coverage of the Warriors this season will be unprecedented in scope. (Anda Chu/Staff)

13

"I don't want to walk in the door thinking about Game 7," Curry said, referring to defeat last June 19 that capped the Cavs' comeback from down 3-1.

"Nobody should be thinking that way. But you should remember how you felt when you were walking off the floor. You should remember all that you did all summer to get yourself in a better position individually and collectively."

This year's Warriors will feature a quartet of All-Stars: Curry, Durant, Green and Klay Thompson.

They are basketball's Beatles — the Fab Four-iors — complete with the hype. But they insisted Monday that they are ready for hoopla.

"We're used to the pressure," reserve guard Shaun Livingston said. "The stakes will be a lot higher this year than they were last year, just because of adding Kevin and the team that we have in place. But I've been on nine teams, and I know that there are worse situations to be in. I'm happy to have all these expectations. You'd rather have it this way than the other way."

Indeed, the chaotic scene prompted Raymond Ridder, the team's longtime vice president of communications, to reflect the bad ol' days. Once upon a time, the Warriors were such a non-story that Ridder and his communications staff would meet before the season and ask themselves: "What can we do to entice people to get interested in our basketball team?"

So they came up with gimmicks. One year, reporters could meet at Monta Ellis' house and hitch a ride to the press conference.

Any bright ideas this year?

"This year, the idea was: 'I'm sorry, you can't come,'" Ridder cracked.

Far from the days of hitching a ride with a player, Tim Bontemps of the *Washington Post* drove himself across the country. He piled into his 2009 Dodge Avenger last week and began high-tailing it across the country, 11-hours at a time.

For Bontemps, it was a one-way trip. He is one of several national reporters moving to the Bay Area for the season to embed with Golden State. *The New York Times*, Bleacher Report, *USA Today* and ESPN are also planning to cover the Warriors on a frequent basis.

"I really think the Warriors are going to be the dominant story line in sports over the next nine months," Bontemps said. "When you look at the American sporting landscape between now and June, it's hard for me to see a bigger story than what's going on with the Warriors on a daily basis."

But this year's Warriors tale has already taken a darker twist. They are no longer the cuddly Globetrotter clones featuring a Baby-Faced Assassin.

Critics now cast them as overrated chokers who became the first team in NBA history to blow a 3-to-1 lead in the Finals. The Warriors also lost their tempers along the way, with Curry chucking his mouth guard into the stands and Green emerging as a threat to groins everywhere.

Signing Durant to a two-year, $54.275 million deal in the offseason had the dual effect of creating a super-team and robbing

Steph Curry drives to the hoop against teammate Ian Clark during practice in Oakland. (Anda Chu/Staff)

Kevin Durant and Steph Curry will be among the most potent scoring duos in NBA history. (Jane Tyska/Staff)

Oklahoma City of the most beloved star it has ever known.

"Listen, the Warriors are going to be the most hated team in the NBA this year. They're also going to be the most popular team," Bontemps said. "Every arena they go to, they're going to get booed unmercifully. And everyone across the country who is a neutral fan is going to be rooting against them.

"It's just the way our society works, right? It's just a lot more fun to see a Goliath get taken down."

Sam Amick, who covers the NBA for *USA Today*, has already felt reader backlash. He recently scored an extensive one-on-one interview with Curry, and parlayed that sit-down into several stories.

"And every single time I tweeted something about the story, there was some non-Warriors fan chiming in to say 'Whatever, they blew a 3-1 lead' — or even something more vulgar," Amick said. "Today I blocked a guy because he had something X-rated to say about Steph. ... Certain fans resent the hype and the way (the Warriors) were talked about as an invincible team."

In the least, the Warriors seemed prepared for the media day onslaught, which was no small feat considering it's turned into a three-hour gamut. The itinerary included required stops at the Warriors social media hub, where players goofed around on Instagram, Facebook, Twitter and Snapchat and other apps born long after Bob Cousy.

Next up? The actual basketball part. Practice starts tomorrow at 11 a.m.

"This day is always weird," Curry said. "There are always a lot of emotions and thoughts on this day because it marks the start of a new year. It's weird, but I know we're excited."

# READY TO ROLL

## Steph Curry Primed for Redemption

By Marcus Thompson II | September 26, 2016

The highlight of Stephen Curry's summer was a party in New York City, a climactic end to a frantic offseason.

In hindsight, as he flipped through his memories of the past few months, he most fondly remembered two-stepping at an exclusive shindig last week on the second floor of William Sonoma. The summer saw him play golf with President Obama again, help land Kevin Durant, tour Asia and even drive an IndyCar at Sonoma Raceway.

But this party was most grand because of the occasion.

"We celebrated my wife's New York book tour," Curry said after his session at Warriors media day. "We had a blast. It was a special moment."

Another summer, another whirlwind for Curry.

This time, Curry was the supporting actor. He still had appearances, commercial shoots and basketball camps. But on top of that, he was riding along Ayesha Curry's whirlwind as she released her new cookbook.

These chaotic offseasons have proven to be a good thing for Curry. The storm forces him to find the calm. The burdensome schedule makes him diligent about not neglecting his duties.

His workouts become therapy. Basketball becomes his sanctuary from the demands of stardom. So as usual, Curry comes to training camp in shape, healthy and revved up.

The offseason is work. But now starts the love.

"This thing is always weird," Curry said. "No matter how your season ends, it's always — a lot of different emotions and thoughts that go into this day, because it does mark the start of a new year."

Curry said he is healthy. The medial collateral ligament in his right knee is

After the Golden State Warriors' heartbreaking collapse in the 2016 NBA Finals, Steph Curry is ready for another shot at victory. (Aric Crabb/Staff)

# The limited player whom millions watched underwhelm in the NBA Finals is gone, and back should be the two-time MVP.

healed. His conditioning is on point. The limited player whom millions watched underwhelm in the NBA Finals is gone, and back should be the two-time MVP.

He is no stranger to summers packed with special events. Talk shows. Endorsement obligations. Product endorsements. Flights all over. Those are par for the course when you're the MVP and face of a franchise that's become the face of the NBA. This is his new norm. For at least the past few years, something major has happened to dominate his offseason.

But underneath the special events and appearances is usually a mission. That never seems to get lost in all the offseason fun. He usually has something driving him while all the spoils of his celebrity figure to distract him.

In 2012, he was recovering from career-threatening ankle surgery. He worked like never before to prove his career wasn't doomed.

In 2013, he left Nike and became the face of Under Armour, and mixed in a trip to Tanzania, Africa, to pass out malaria nets in person. But he also had to prove he was ready to lead the Warriors to another level after they upset Denver in the first round and fought tough against San Antonio.

In 2014, he played in the FIBA World Cup of Basketball. He went to Spain an All-Star

and face of the rising Warriors, but lost out to Chris Paul in a grueling seven-game series. He then played a second-tier role with Team USA. Curry was determined to prove he was elite.

In 2015, he was the MVP and an NBA champion. He was the face of basketball. His new bent became justifying the hype.

In 2016, his wife became a celebrity chef, author and television persona.

"They're both just amazing experiences because they're things we never dreamt of doing," Curry said. "They're things that (are) our passions, like I love playing basketball, she loves doing what she does in the kitchen, making recipes and connecting with people. It's all pretty natural. But it's different being on the other side, for sure. I enjoyed that part of it. Just kind of watching."

The watching is over. Curry ended the season in the most heartbreaking of fashions: playing his worst game of the season in the biggest game of the year.

History tells us Curry will be driven by the Warriors' Game 7 collapse, by many doubting what he's accomplished.

History tells us before the all the fun he had this offseason, the media tours and once-in-a-lifetime experiences, he was working toward vindicating his name.

The offseason is work. Now starts the love. 🏀

Steph Curry and his wife Ayesha talk about their ride after experiencing a lap in an IndyCar driven by Mario Andretti before the Indy Grand Prix of Sonoma. It was a busy offseason for Curry on and off the court, as he prepared to defend his consecutive NBA MVP awards. (Jose Carlos Fajardo/Staff)

# BACK TO BUSINESS

## Kevin Durant Begins New Chapter with the Warriors

### By Anthony Slater | September 26, 2016

The Warriors set up a massive press conference room for media day. Rows of desks were surrounded by piles of overflow chairs. Cords slithered everywhere. Cameras lined a platform in the back, pointed at a larger platform in the front, where player after player circulated through.

Kevin Durant batted eighth, the most anticipated hitter buried deep in the lineup. He strolled to the podium with a smile, then folded into his seat, the next small step in his new world. The optics remain a bit strange.

Behind Durant, three banners rose about 10 feet over his head, for background visual purposes. Each had 77 Warriors logos plastered on them, 231 in all, as if the organization was screaming at your eyeballs: 'Yeah, remember, he plays for us now.'

"It's real," Durant said, a 232nd Warrior logo planted on the front of his No. 35 jersey.

But Durant isn't a newbie to the game. He's a media day veteran. Media day wasn't much different. KD zipped from station to station, autographing basketballs, sliding behind some curtains for radio voiceovers and navigating through various photo stations. He's long transformed from athlete to brand. This is his comfort zone.

The press conference had a few more people than his previous media days in middle America. But the NBA megastar has faced crowds far deeper and been asked questions far more stressful.

"It's about the same, to be honest," Durant said. "Doing the same things, the same coverage."

Media day was easy. The next day begins business. It's everything outside of that building to which he's still adjusting. This wasn't the easiest summer for Durant to

Since dominating offseason headlines by signing with the Warriors, Kevin Durant has won an Olympic gold medal and prepared with his new teammates for the long road ahead. (Aric Crabb/Staff)

make a mid-career leap. He barely had any time for the move or acclimation.

A few days after signing, he held an introductory press conference on July 7. He was in the Bay less than a day. Then he was off to Asia for more than a week. Then it was to Vegas for Team USA camp and Rio for the Olympics. He made a quick pitstop at Oracle for an exhibition, but that was brief and hectic.

By the time the Olympics were over, his offseason was almost dead. He had to squeeze out a final few trips, for both business and pleasure. He popped up in Greece for a vacation, Austin for a leadership conference, Washington D.C., his home, for a Redskins game and both Seattle and Madison, Wisconsin, for some charity work.

Durant's been a Warrior for nearly three months. But only a handful of those days have actually been spent in the Bay Area. He's still settling into his Oakland Hills home. Life without air conditioning, like for many around the Bay the last couple days, has been brutal.

"My life will change just because I'm in a different city," Durant said. "I think that's probably the only thing. My game? We'll see."

The offseason has provided plenty of stress for Durant, but also time for his life-altering decision to settle. Perspective comes when you visit a maximum-security prison like San Quentin, which Durant did recently. Realization comes during those quiet times on his countless flights.

"It's just become more and more realistic as each day goes by," he said.

Venom likely awaits Durant in almost every opposing city this offseason. He gets a taste of it any time he opens social media these days. In a recent interview on HBO's Any Given Wednesday, that backlash seemed to have formed a defiant edge in Durant as camped loomed.

Maybe it did. But KD tried not to show it at media day. He's known to be moody with reporters, but at media day that mood was generally pleasant. He was gracious before and after his press conference and upbeat during it.

"It's new, fresh and I'm looking forward to it," Durant said of his new venture. "I just got super excited as I was walking in here. Just to play here and play for this great organization and play with these players, I'm excited."

Minor jabs still seem to irk him. A reporter asked whether he'd have joined the Warriors had they won the title. "They didn't," Durant quickly shot back.

But even though some players thrive with that extra edge – and Durant certainly has at times in the past – KD says he's not searching for fuel from the outside.

"I always play with passion," Durant said. "But my thing is just playing for myself. I don't want to go out there and play upset with everybody else. I want to play my game and enjoy the game of basketball"

A huge adjustment period lies ahead. But a chunk of that may have more to do with his new life off the court. On it, his teammates are pretty confident he'll fit in well.

"There were some holes on our team (last year)," Andre Iguodala said. "We got a monster to fill them all."

Now teammates, Kevin Durant and Stephen Curry represent the last three years of NBA regular-season MVP winners.
(Aric Crabb/Staff)

# LOCKED IN

## With Stephen Curry and Kevin Durant, Warriors Present the Ultimate Quandary to Defenses

### By Marcus Thompson II | October 6, 2016

Klay Thompson said he wasn't going to sacrifice his game because the Warriors have Kevin Durant. It sounded as if Thompson might have been revealing the first sign of trouble on the Warriors' super team, as if he wasn't willing to share the ball. But his declaration might be quite prophetic.

The Warriors are so loaded on offense, he might end up getting more shots. With all the attention teams will have to pay to Durant and Stephen Curry, Thompson could reap the rewards of lesser defenders and defensive lapses.

He's already getting all the shots he wants. Think about it: Thompson, a two-time All-Star and second-team All-NBA selection, being guarded by a team's third-best defender or getting left alone in a game of "Pick Your Poison." The Warriors still have Draymond Green, Andre Iguodala and Shaun Livingston, and Ian Clark is looking like he's ready for a bigger role.

How can this team be guarded?

That might be the question that determines everything this season. Much of the talk is about how they will mesh and who will get the shots. But more pressing is what's the scheme to stop this varied attack? That's the question the Los Angeles Clippers left Oracle asking on Tuesday, comforted only by the insignificance of the game.

Last year, the plan was to load up on Curry. He was the head of the snake and was met with double-teams and traps and physical play. The secondary defender would

Kevin Durant drives past center DeAndre Jordan during the Warriors' 120-75 preseason rout of the Los Angeles Clippers. (Jane Tyska/Staff)

then be on Thompson and the opponent would pray that's enough.

With this new lineup, if they trap Curry, that leaves Durant one-on-one. And helping on him gives open looks to Thompson and Green.

The other option is to not trap Curry, which will lead to the same results that prompted the trap in the first place.

Again: how can this team be guarded?

Kevin Durant solves several of the scoring issues the Warriors had late last season.

The Warriors' top six players have so many options, so many ways to attack.

They can put Livingston or Iguodala at point guard and have Curry, Durant, Thompson and Green running off screens and setting them.

They can run their trusty pick-and-roll with Green and Curry, and have Durant on one side and Thompson on the other, forcing the defense to stay home or help and give them open shots.

They can run the offense through Durant and flank him with the two best shooters in the game, giving him space to drive because defenses are terrified of the Splash Brothers catching fire.

Above: Trapping Steph Curry still leaves Kevin Durant, Klay Thompson and Draymond Green open to do damage.
Opposite: Green dunks against the Clippers at Oracle Arena in Oakland. (Jane Tyska/Staff)

# Durant gives the Warriors what they didn't have — someone who can counter physicality by getting to the free-throw line.

"Yeah. This team potentially could be better than any team in NBA history," said two-time MVP Steve Nash, who has been working out with players at Warriors practice. "But again, that's just potential. They have to find a way to play together. If they can find that, sure, they can be the best offensive team ever."

For this you can be sure: the NBA will figure something out. It may not be this year. But eventually, the bright and creative minds, whose entire existence is devoted to schematics and strategy, will come up with something.

The Cavaliers came up with a plan to defend the Warriors, though aided by circumstances: press up and take away the open 3s, grab and hold until the whistle blows, and force the supporting cast to beat them. It worked. Curry and Thompson settled for contested 3-pointers against the pressure defense. Harrison Barnes went ice cold. The bench couldn't score.

But now the Warriors have Durant. In addition to giving the Warriors one more player who can't be left open, Durant gives the Warriors what they didn't have — someone who can counter physicality by getting to the free-throw line.

The likelihood early is that teams will switch after every screen on defense.

Instead of creating openings, mismatches and numbers advantages for the Warriors by trapping or fighting through screens, coach Steve Kerr is expecting teams to switch. Oklahoma City did it in the Western Conference Finals with success. So did Cleveland.

The Warriors employ the same defense. The trick, though, is personnel. It works when the defense has five players who are comfortable defending any position. Not many teams have that. Most of those that do will be going away from its lineup when it faces the Warriors.

Kerr is preparing for that defense already. The Warriors don't have plays. Kerr doesn't like thick playbooks. Instead, he likes philosophies and sets with multiple options. The key for the Warriors will be reading where the advantages are on the court. Durant has been working on his post game so when a point guard switches onto him, he can take advantage. Green has been working on his mid-range game so he can take his bigger defender and stick the pull-up or floater.

If the switch-everything approach doesn't work, most teams will be leaving a game against the Warriors just like the Clippers. Completely defeated. 🏀

Klay Thompson's quick shooting makes defending this Warriors team a significant challenge. (Jane Tyska/Staff)

# SUMMER LIKE
# NO OTHER

# MOTIVATION

## Curry, Iguodala Don't Intend to Forget

### By Tim Kawakami | June 19, 2016

There, at the end, Stephen Curry and Andre Iguodala just froze in place, like they were stuck in a moment that should have never happened.

That seemed to be occurring in an impossible dimension with an unimaginable conclusion.

Until right then, until this Warriors dream season was over, frittered away, failed, and then fading to black.

The buzzer for Game 7 sounded, the Warriors lost 93-89, Oracle Arena went silent except for the exclamations of the Cavaliers, and Curry and Iguodala just stood there as most of their teammates filed off the court and back into the locker room.

They waited. They witnessed. Eventually, they congratulated the Cavaliers players and coaches they could.

It was over — the Warriors' 73-victory regular season, the playoff journey, the 3-1 lead in this Finals series, this operatic game.

And somebody else was triumphant, somebody else played better, coached better, played harder, and deserved it.

Somebody who was not the Warriors, who became the first team in Finals history to lose after taking a 3-1 lead.

"Yeah, it stung," Curry said later of those minutes watching LeBron James & Co. scream and hug. "It sucked to watch them celebrate, and we wish that would have been us.

"But at the end of the day, you congratulate them for accomplishing what they set out to do, and it will be a good image for us over the summer and all next season to remember so that we can come back stronger."

Failing to beat the Cleveland Cavaliers after taking a 3-1 series lead in the Finals serves as painful, powerful motivation for this Warriors team. (Jose Carlos Fajardo/Staff)

The Warriors, though, were supposed to be the strongest team in the league and maybe one of the strongest teams in NBA history.

They were supposed to back up last season's championship with another title this season, they were supposed to finish off Cleveland again.

But Draymond Green was suspended for Game 5, which Cleveland won with gargantuan performances by James and Kyrie Irving, and the Warriors never pried back the momentum from there.

That carried through Game 6 in Cleveland and all the way into the fourth quarter, when the Warriors edged ahead, but their offense broke down — missing their last nine shots.

Then Irving hit a humongous 3-pointer over Curry with 53 seconds left, and the Warriors fell short one last time.

"You know, we've had so many moments of joy together, and it was like, wow, we're actually having a moment of sorrow as a team," coach Steve Kerr said.

Impossible. Unthinkable. That was the reaction of the Oracle fans, and that was the

Fans look on as head coach Steve Kerr and general manager Bob Myers leave the court following the Warriors' 93-89 Game 7 NBA Finals defeat. (Nhat V. Meyer/Staff)

reaction — for a while — in the Warriors' locker room afterward.

And now the Warriors are pushed into the category of greatest teams to fall short of a title — there with the 2007 New England Patriots and the 2001 Seattle Mariners.

Curry, the first-ever unanimous regular-season MVP, was outplayed by LeBron and Irving in the final three games, and while Green redeemed himself with a tremendous Game 7 effort, it was not enough.

"We're stunned," Kerr said. "We thought we were going to win. I was extremely confident coming into tonight, especially having Draymond back from the suspension from 5 and now 7, Game 7, at home.

"But this is why you can't mess around. Not that we messed around, but this is why every game counts.

"Game 5 was really the key. That was the turning point of the whole series."

In Game 7, the Warriors' last score was with 4:39 left, which is a stunning concept for such a powerful offensive team.

But not out of line with the way this series turned in Game 5 and some of the weaknesses the Warriors displayed at times this postseason.

Once Andrew Bogut was lost to a knee injury Game 5, Kerr struggled to put a center out there he could trust and the Warriors suffered for it.

He forced Festus Ezeli and Anderson Varejao into this game, and they both struggled, with Ezeli's short stint in the fourth quarter a particular turning point.

But that was the fascinating part of the Warriors' "Strength in Numbers"

credo — they had many great players and achievements, yet in the end they ran out.

So is this a failed season after the record 24-0 start, the awards, the raucous times at Oracle? An empty journey?

"Obviously everybody will say, oh, man, they won 73 but they didn't win a championship," Green said. "We didn't. But I think this team accomplished a lot of great things individually and as a team, and those things can never be taken away …

"We didn't reach the end prize, but there will be more years for that."

That was part of the reason Green said he came back out onto the court during Cleveland's celebration after he first went into the Warriors' locker room.

He wanted to pay respects to the Cavaliers, but he also wanted to remember. So did Curry.

They're the two players who have led the Warriors during this entire amazing two-season run, and they wanted to be present at the worst possible point of it.

"We want to keep this memory so that it will fuel us as we stay together as a team," Curry said.

"Because like Draymond said, this ain't the last time you're going to see us on this stage."

Afterward, Cleveland danced, while Curry, Iguodala and Green wished they were anywhere else in the universe.

But they stayed. They witnessed. They flashed back to a year ago, when they were the ones celebrating, and they flashed ahead a year, when they badly want to do it again. 🏀

# THE DURANT DREAM COMES TRUE

## Warriors Add Superstar, Assemble Transcendent Starting Five

By Tim Kawakami | July 4, 2016

For at least two years, Joe Lacob and Bob Myers plotted and planned and hoped and juggled salaries and, yes, believed that the Warriors could land Kevin Durant to create an ultimate NBA dynasty.

They dreamed. They got signs that it was possible over the last few years and months, but just signs. Just glimmers and whispers.

They didn't know it for sure, because nobody knew how Durant would finally decide this, and what the final factors would be.

But the Warriors' top executives always believed they had the most compelling case to this most-prized free agent — they believed Durant's loyalty to Oklahoma City was powerful, but the best basketball and post-basketball decision would always be the Warriors.

They had to hold their breath, they had Jerry West talk to Durant as their ultimate deal-closer, then they had to wait it out just like everybody else. But then, the gargantuan news landed:

Kevin Durant is coming to the Warriors on a two-year, $54.3M deal (per ESPN's Marc Stein on the terms), with an ability to opt out next July.

OK. Stop. This is obviously humongous, a potential era-changing moment not just for the Warriors, but for the entire league, and this is exactly what they sold him on.

If Durant wants to become an NBA legend and reset the league as we know it, he comes

Andre Iguodala shoots over Kevin Durant in Game 5 of the 2016 Western Conference finals against the Thunder. (Nhat V. Meyer/Staff)

to the Warriors and turns them into one of the most amazing rosters ever assembled, and that's what he just did.

How did this happen? It happened because the Warriors have built themselves into exactly the kind of franchise that a star like Durant would want to join.

It happened because the Warriors won 73 games and were 50 seconds from a title a few weeks ago ... while still maintaining the cap flexibility to sign Durant to a max deal.

It happened because Stephen Curry, Draymond Green and Andre Iguodala are friends with Durant and have been tacitly or more than tacitly recruiting Durant for a while, even through that torrid seven-game Western Conference final.

It happened because West hit the precise point at the precisely right time: If Durant can't win a championship in OKC, and it was looking like he might not, why not make the move when he is at his absolute prime to join a team that has proven it can win a title and is set up to win many more?

Durant told the Warriors throughout the process that he liked their franchise more than any other.

He told them he wanted to play with Curry & Co., and he loved Steve Kerr's system, and the Silicon Valley sensibilities of Joe Lacob's front office.

But he always told the Warriors he wasn't sure if he could leave OKC because of everything that had been built there, and because of his loyalties to Westbrook and others.

As of Sunday night, maybe even into Monday morning, Warriors executives were still not sure if they were going to convince him to make the jump.

But they believed they were the right fit for Durant, if he wants to be a part of a dynasty, and he finally agreed.

Around the Warriors the last few weeks, the working idea has been that if they landed Durant, they would start the most lethal five in NBA history (theoretically): Durant, Curry, Klay Thompson, Green and Iguodala.

The Warriors all but physically set that up when they sent Curry, Klay, Draymond and Iguodala to the meeting with Durant in The Hamptons.

Four guys. Durant was the fifth. Get it?

The Warriors must now renounce almost all of their free agents (absolutely Harrison Barnes and Festus Ezeli) and trade Andrew Bogut (sources say he's headed to the Mavericks) and get no money in return in order to clear max space.

As for the rest of the Warriors' bench?

They have Shaun Livingston, Kevon Looney, the draft picks Damian Jones and Patrick McCaw... and then it gets a little tricky.

The Warriors don't have to renounce all of their free agents, but the only ones they can possibly bring back are the cheapest ones — Ian Clark and James Michael McAdoo — and maybe Kerr will prevail and get Leandro Barbosa back on a minimum deal.

There are some salary-cap sleight-of-hand scenarios ... but generally, the Warriors will have to fill out the rest of their roster using only the $2.9M room exception and then minimum salaries.

And they will need at least one center and maybe two.

With Durant clearly planning to opt out next summer, are the Warriors in jeopardy of losing him then?

It's a practical possibility, but not likely: He told them he was making a long-term decision, even if he signed short-term (to take advantage of the cap spike).

Also, the Warriors have many ways to pay him his max next July, even combined with an expected $30M-plus per season contract for Curry.

If the chemistry is good and the team plays well next season, there is no reason to think that Durant would want to go through this again and bail on the Warriors.

This was his choice for history. This was his choice to chase titles for the rest of his career. This was the choice the Warriors set themselves up for him to make, and he made it. 🏀

A recent formidable opponent as part of the Oklahoma City Thunder, Kevin Durant signed on in July to pursue an NBA title with the Warriors instead. (Aric Crabb/Staff)

# THE NEW VILLAINS

## Kevin Durant Makes Warriors Most Hated Team in League

By Marcus Thompson II | July 4, 2016

After winning the Kevin Durant sweepstakes, the Warriors have the kind of talent to become one of the greatest teams of all time. Dare we say "light years" ahead of the competition?

They are already the first to have the last two MVPs together, with Durant having won the award before Stephen Curry took the next two. The Warriors now have four players from the latest All-NBA teams, including Draymond Green and Klay Thompson on the second team.

But in order to maximize their unheralded potential, the Warriors will have to manage their new reality: They will be one of the most hated teams in the NBA.

They need to embrace it.

Oh, you thought they were villains last year? Watch the exponential increase in venom thrown their way this year. Durant jerseys are already ablaze in Oklahoma City.

There is a natural balance to these things in normal circumstances. The more a sports figure is beloved, the more inevitable it is that a contingent of haters will arrive. But the Warriors getting Durant is like a millionaire winning the lottery. The rich getting richer, and that will turn the vitriol up for sure.

So, here is the early question about these supercharged Warriors: Can they handle the black hat?

"In most arenas, we had a strong contingent of Warriors fans," Curry said. "But as far as being hated, all the noise stays out of our locker room. We focus on what we have to do. We have experience dealing with it. We were the villains (in the Finals) so we

Draymond Green can teach Kevin Durant a thing or two about being viewed as a villain by opposing fans.
(Jane Tyska/Staff)

will be more prepared. But all that matters is what goes on in our locker room."

Not that long ago, the Warriors were the epitome of lovable. A bunch of nice-guy underdogs who had obvious fun and played an entertaining style of basketball. Those days were clearly over after they won a championship, followed by their chase for 73 turning them into one of the most hyped teams ever.

CEO Joe Lacob's comments about the Warriors being "light years" ahead of the NBA gave credence to the anti-Warriors crowd's bemoans of arrogance. People grew weary of the Warriors and their rampant love. The once-cute, inspirational, play-the-game-the-right-way squad that brought beauty back to basketball officially became antagonists.

That was never more evident when the Warriors choked away a 3-1 lead in the NBA Finals. It was hard to tell if some were more happy about the Warriors' demise or impressed by the Cavaliers' impressive feat.

Now, the Warriors add one of the league's top players to the mix. They have arguably the two best players in the league not named LeBron James. The Warriors are going to be received with the affection of Darth Vader — after a video leak of him kicking a poodle.

Can you imagine the jeering that will happen when the Warriors and Durant return to Oklahoma City?

The hatred was already epic in Cleveland during the Finals. Just ask the family

Head coach Steve Kerr has an enviable amount of talent at his disposal with the addition of Kevin Durant.
(Jane Tyska/Staff)

members of Warriors players who made the trip. San Antonio will shower the Warriors in fury. Houston fans have even more reason to despise the Warriors, who knocked their Rockets out of the last two postseasons.

Portland fans will have a special beef after the Warriors eliminated the Blazers. Dallas, which can't get a top free agent to save Mark Cuban's life and still remembers "We Believe," will unleash their jealous rage.

And when they go play the Clippers ... well, the Warriors fans usually take over Staples, so never mind.

But winning for the Warriors will require growing comfortable in hostility. They can't be the team to fall apart on the road as they did multiple times in the playoffs. Because those environments — like it was in Oklahoma City in Games 3 and 4, and Cleveland in Games 3 and 6 — will be closer to the norm. They will need to take a special joy in silencing those crowds, like in Game 6 at OKC and Game 3 in Cleveland.

Few NBA teams have received the kind of backlash the Warriors will. The Heat had to deal with this when LeBron teamed up with Dwyane Wade and Chris Bosh.

Who else has such a large jeer section? You'd probably have to go back to the '90s for those great Bulls teams and the Bad Boy Pistons. But the NBA wasn't big enough then, nor the coverage multifaceted enough, for the dislike to spread like a contagion.

The disdain for these Warriors might eclipse that of The Heatles — especially since we are even further along in the age of social media, where vitriol and bullying spread like wildfire, and Hot Take Jakes all over the airwaves. Nuance, context and understanding have been drowned out. There is only Warriors love and Warriors hate.

And the hate will be relentless. With that hate comes weighty pressure. Now, the Warriors' success or failure is national discourse, and not just in sports. Any issues, on and off the court, is now breaking news. Every loss is an I-told-you-so moment for their critics. Falling short of a title is an indictment on them as players.

Can they handle it?

Green, as we know, loves being the villain. This may not be readily apparent, but coach Steve Kerr loves it, too.

Curry rose to MVP status with a love of silencing his skeptics, but these past playoffs were his first as powerful villain, which is much different from underdog. For Durant, being on the receiving end of collective anger will be new.

But their team needs to embrace it, play well with it. Many teams borrow an us-against-the-world mentality. The Warriors need to master it.

Certainly, the Dub Nation will grow, and current members are more fervent in their fandom now that Durant has joined their ranks. That love is what they will return home to. First, they'll have to go shut up a gazillion haters. This is their life now. 🏀

Durant is well-aware of the scrutiny he and his new teammates face in their quest for a championship. (Jane Tyska/Staff)

# BROTHERHOOD

## Chemistry Held Allure for Durant

By Marcus Thompson II | July 7, 2016

Kevin Durant, like many others around the league, suspected the Warriors' players had a great bond. It looks like they have fun, seems like they are close. Durant, though, had to be sure. Before he made this tremendous leap of faith, he wanted to look Stephen Curry in the eyes for an invitation.

But Curry didn't show up alone when he came to the Warriors' meeting with Kevin Durant in the Hamptons last weekend. He had Klay Thompson with him. And Draymond Green. And Andre Iguodala.

Durant said he was shocked the stars of a 73-win would come recruit him. Watched them together, their bond was obvious, genuine. It was symbolism he couldn't ignore.

"To see them together, they all walked in and it looked like they were holding hands," Durant said, prompting laughter from much of the 300 or so people at the introductory news conference. "It was just a family. I could tell they enjoyed being around each other."

The amount of back story in Durant's move could fill a book. And much of the conversation about the Warriors' landmark acquisition has been centered on the reasons he chose to leave Oklahoma City. But this super team that has been formed is as much about what the Warriors have built.

If there is a gist as to what lured Durant to the Bay, it is the chemistry of the Warriors.

Before they were villains, the Warriors were darlings. They overcame their flaws with a collegiate type of chemistry and unselfishness onlookers admired. Their celebrations were heartwarming as they represented what was good about sports.

Stephen Curry and Kevin Durant embrace following Game 7 of the Western Conference finals, just months before the two would become Warriors teammates. (Jose Carlos Fajardo/Staff)

> ## "When I met these guys, I felt as comfortable as I've ever felt. It was organic. It was authentic. It was real."
> ### —Kevin Durant

Over the last couple of years, the Warriors' flaws got diminished by their steadily improving talent and Steve Kerr's system. They stopped looking so heartwarming as they mowed through opponents. Their celebrations drew ire from fans of teams that seemed helpless to stop them.

But what has remained as a staple, even despite the changing climate around the Warriors, was their chemistry.

Yes, on the court. The Warriors led the league in passes and assists, products of a system focused on movement and sharing the ball. Adding Durant to the mix is like putting a turbo boost into the league's best offense. The Warriors will be in the hunt for a championship year after year.

But the chemistry off the court, too, mattered to Durant. In addition to wins and a chance at championships, the Warriors offered him a brotherhood. They offered him to be in a collective of iron that would sharpen his iron.

"We were just ourselves," Curry said in a phone interview. "All we did was pretty much talk. We told him how things would be, how we operated and how he would fit in. He would fit right in. He's a team guy. That's who he really is. We told him he wouldn't have to change anything and we wouldn't have to change anything for him. He just fits right in."

Fit matters to Durant. He emphasized that multiple times. And the Warriors convinced him by simply displaying how they roll.

Before the meeting, they huddled and reiterated their plan to not say anything negative about Oklahoma City. Their plan was to simply showcase themselves.

As has been reported, part of the meeting was just the players. Durant and the Warriors' four huddled and chatted. They answered his questions, detailed the inner workings of the franchise, painted the real picture from a player's perspective.

The bond that Durant saw, even up close as the Warriors came back from a 3-1 series deficit against Durant's Thunder, felt real.

It was a feeling he couldn't ignore.

"When I met these guys," he said, "I felt as comfortable as I've ever felt. It was organic. It was authentic. It was real."

It's going to take incredible chemistry to handle what the Warriors have coming. The hype that followed them will be significantly increased. The pressure to win will be as heavy as ever. And Durant is already getting destroyed in the court of public opinion, which includes former players and analysts.

What's more, the Warriors won't have the depth people have come to expect. With two spots remaining, the Warriors' bench is a question mark.

But this season, and the next several, isn't about the bench. It's about Durant, Curry, Klay Thompson, Green, Iguodala and Shaun Livingston being greater than the rest of the league. They will have to carry this team. They will have to push each other to be better. They will have to shoulder the expectations.

For most of the last eight years, Durant has felt the heft of championship pressure. But it was all on him and guard Russell Westbrook.

And then the Warriors came and showed him how different it could be. How much lighter the weight is when more share the burden. How much better basketball is when bonding is at the core.

"I just saw a bunch of real guys. Simple as that," Durant said. "It felt like they weren't in the NBA. It felt like those guys just play pickup every single day and they just really enjoy pure basketball. That's the kind of feel that I wanted."

And it was a desire he couldn't ignore.

Kevin Durant talks with Golden State Warriors head coach Steve Kerr, general manager Bob Myers and assistant coach Ron Adams. (Aric Crabb/Staff)

# SHOOTING FOR GREATNESS

## Durant Comfortable with Decision to Join Warriors

By Tim Kawakami | July 7, 2016

Kevin Durant wanted a basketball in his hands, and he wanted to shoot.

A little earlier, Durant wore a sleek suit, strode on stage at the Warriors' practice site, and cheerily moved through all the proper public paces after signing the two-year, $54.3 million deal with the Warriors that shook the league.

But now, a few dozen minutes after the media barrage, one of the greatest scorers in history wanted to shoot. He was back in sweats, surrounded by friends, relaxed, refreshed, and he wanted to make the ball go through the net at the Warriors' practice court.

"Let's see if my three-ball is working," Durant announced, before a swish, and another, and a few more.

Then he missed one, and Warriors general manager Bob Myers called out, joking: "Hey, we don't miss shots on this team!"

Durant just laughed and nodded, and pumped a few more in, stepping backward and backward, almost to half-court, and the ball kept going through the net.

This was the new scourge of the NBA, the man who enraged the entire state of Oklahoma and infuriated the league after leaving the Thunder to join the Warriors' collection of stars.

But Durant seemed completely at peace as he put up those shots, just as comfortable as he was answering questions and explaining why, at 27, he had decided to move west and join Stephen Curry & Co.

Kevin Durant understood that, in joining the Warriors, he would open himself up to new, league-wide criticism.
(Jose Carlos Fajardo/Staff)

53

# "We live in this superhero comic book world where either you're a villain or you're a superhero if you're in this position, and I know that."
## —Kevin Durant

It was about that basketball and that rim — about being happy, about success, about comfort and about committing to that decision.

And if Durant was shocked or flustered by the fusillade of criticism, he showed no signs of it.

In fact, he said he figured this would happen.

"I knew the dance was about to start," Durant said of his feelings once he decided to go to the Warriors. "I knew it was coming."

So, instead of sounding defensive and resentful, Durant just repeated that he knew the Warriors were the right team for him.

He thought he could be the "missing piece of the puzzle" after they barely missed a chance for back-to-back championships, and he said that he was ready for a new challenge.

Would he have come here if the Warriors were the two-time defending champions?

"They weren't, though, you know?" Durant said. "They weren't. Who knows. We can talk about hypotheticals all day. But they weren't.

"That's one thing I saw as well — they were so hungry to get back to where they were. Obviously they won 73 games. But they didn't really care about that."

Curry, Draymond Green, Andre Iguodala and Klay Thompson just wanted to add Durant so they could win more titles and enjoy the journey together. Durant wanted that exactly.

Owner Joe Lacob, Myers, coach Steve Kerr: All the same, all on the same page, as Lacob told Durant at the Warriors' presentation in The Hamptons in New York last weekend.

The funny thing, Durant said, is that he's being accused of taking the easy way out.

No, Durant said, it's the opposite for him personally — he has to move his family out from Oklahoma City after eight years, he has to figure out where to live and how this all will work on and off the court.

But that's also what seems to energize him about this — if it felt easier, it probably would've been the wrong decision.

And if Durant and the Warriors are destined to be considered NBA super-villains this season and for all seasons they're together, he seemed fairly reasonable about it.

He used to be one of the league's good guys; maybe he can take a lot of people thinking he is the opposite now.

"We live in this superhero comic book world where either you're a villain or you're a superhero if you're in this position, and I know that," Durant said.

"And I know I haven't changed as a person. I don't treat people any differently because I made the decision to play basketball in another city.

"I understand the fans in Oklahoma City and basketball fans around the world are, I guess, upset, but like I said, I made the decision based upon what I wanted to do and how I felt, and it's the best decision for me."

So yes, Durant seemed like a man who had picked up his things and moved far from his old home, but liked where he was.

And even though he plans to opt out of this deal next July, that's merely to take advantage of the larger money available then. Which the Warriors will pay.

"I don't want to go through that again," Durant said of open free agency. "I plan on being here. I'm committed.

"I'm looking forward to a new era of basketball for me, personally, and it should be fun."

Durant, against the odds, had fun on Thursday, in his suit and in sweats, answering questions and firing up long-distance jumpers.

He was comfortable. He was eager. And the ball kept going through the net, again and again.

Kevin Durant is flanked by general manager Bob Myers and head coach Steve Kerr during his introductory press conference. (Jane Tyska/Staff)

# THE NEW EDDIE D

## Lacob's Transformation of Warriors Reminds Some of 49ers Glory Days

By Tim Kawakami | July 5, 2016

One former longtime member of the 49ers organization from the Eddie DeBartolo Jr. days texted me a little bit after Kevin Durant announced he was signing with the Warriors to say this:

"What the Warriors did reminded me of what 49ers used to do. (Joe) Lacob is Bay Area's new Mr. D."

I checked in with another veteran of those days with that idea and he just said: "Yep."

Maybe that just sounds like normal conversation, but if you know how much 49ers people from those days revere Eddie D, and how much they enjoyed those moments (and, most dramatically, his signing of Deion Sanders to set up the 1994 Super Bowl run), you know this is not said lightly by anybody associated with those times.

If these guys are saying Lacob is becoming the new Eddie D — and obviously, there are many more titles to be won before the Lacob/Peter Guber Warriors can be truly comparable to the five-trophy 49ers Dynasty — then everybody else can contemplate it, too.

Because it is happening, and Durant's arrival is the loudest crackle and bang to signify it.

You don't have to be enamored with Joe Lacob's style, or his "light-years" declarations, or his aggressive front office, or the Silicon Valley venture capitalist credo, or the ticket prices, or the intended move to San Francisco, or any of it, if you wish.

You might love it, too — whatever. That's not the point right now.

Majority owner Joe Lacob has transformed the Warriors from a lackluster franchise into a team with dynastic potential.
(Jose Carlos Fajardo/Staff)

This is about what I always point to when I discuss Lacob and Peter Guber. ...

Don't get stuck on what you hear or see from them on camera or on speaking panels, look at what they're doing, look at the rebuild of the Warriors franchise, look at what they inherited, and look at what they have now.

They bought the team in 2010 after Chris Cohan had run this franchise into the ground, burned the surrounding hillsides, and pillaged everything he could take.

When Lacob/Guber took over, no good player wanted to be part of this and the bad ones wanted to be overpaid to be a part of it.

They had Curry — drafted in 2009, against his wishes — they had Don Nelson under contract, and that's about all they had.

And now: It's a franchise that has built up a young core that had been lobbying Durant for months, had his ear, flew out to the meeting together, and convinced Durant that he had no other choice but to join what was going on here.

It's a franchise that had Bob Myers, who kept the books flexible enough to do this, and it had Steve Kerr and a coaching staff that Durant could embrace.

Joe Lacob looks on from the sidelines during Game 5 of the 2016 Finals against the Cleveland Cavaliers. (Jose Carlos Fajardo/Staff)

Finally, it's a franchise that had Jerry West for the final push, in a telephone conversation with Durant, and none of the other contenders had anything like that.

If Lacob were as bombastic and terrifying to work for as some believe ... would these players, coaches and executives fight so hard to add to his franchise? No, they would not.

And some of the same people actually defended Cohan and Robert Rowell back in the 2000s — I never understood why — and you can ask: What great players and executives did they have fighting for them?

None. They had none.

Again, you don't have to love Lacob's braggadocio or audacity, but if you don't have that, I don't think you plot for two years for Durant, and then land him, or swing for Dwight Howard three years ago and land Andre Iguodala as a secondary plan.

If you don't aim for the highest goals possible, you will never achieve those things, and if Lacob at times has looked a little reckless doing it ... he will take it, the team will take it, his employees will take it, and Durant just embraced it in a moment he could've gone to any team in the league.

I recently asked a Warriors official if the team was ready to become supervillains by signing Durant.

Answer: "Aren't we considered villains already?"

The Warriors person meant that they've been the marquee team for two years and others always want to knock off the marquee team. Now, of course, that'll be amplified

Joe Lacob and Steve Kerr are unfazed by the Warriors' new identity as NBA villains. (Nhat V. Meyer/Staff)

even more, especially when they go to OKC, Cleveland, or basically wherever.

But the best team is always a villain on the road. The very best teams are hated.

The Warriors are going to be incredible ... and incredibly hated. And they're OK with that. Because they're audacious enough to have set themselves up to do this for years.

# UNITING A NATION

## Socially Conscious Team USA Hopes to Help Divided Country

### By Marcus Thompson II | July 21, 2016

Team USA breaks every huddle with the same one-word proclamation: United.

The emphasis on team, the feeling of playing for something bigger, is not abnormal come Olympics time. And, normally, an all-black roster in basketball isn't noteworthy.

But given the racial tension in this country, the prevalence of the Black Lives Matter movement, the symbolism is not lost on this group.

"We're going through a tough time right now, in the country and also around the world, and we can provide that sense of togetherness and unity," new Warriors star Kevin Durant said. "Obviously, we definitely want to win a gold medal. That's the most important thing for us as basketball players. But when we look at the big picture of things, we want people to see how much we love each other, see how much we love being around each other. ... We want that united feel when you watch us play. I think having these great group of guys together, you'll see that."

The team representing the United States in the Summer Games in Brazil is all African-American. Again, in basketball, not newsworthy. But, in America, black men are a lightning rod topic. The last few years have been marred with the deaths of several African-American men at the hands of cops, prompting outcry, protests and social media discourse — and backlash. Matters have intensified with police being killed in Dallas and Baton Rouge.

It was enough to make four NBA players — Carmelo Anthony, Chris Paul, LeBron James and Dwyane Wade — hijack the introduction of the ESPYs to deliver a message denouncing violence and encouraging community

United States players stand for the national anthem before the gold medal game against Serbia. (AP Images)

building. That was the latest in several statements NBA players have made regarding race matters.

The Miami Heat took a team photo with hoodies on to show solidarity with Trayvon Martin, a black teen who was killed in 2012. The Los Angeles Clippers took off their warm-up shirts together as a way of denouncing former owner Donald Sterling in mid-2014, and Stephen Curry was planning a Warriors boycott with teammates before Sterling was ousted by the NBA owners. Later that year, Kobe Bryant, Derrick Rose and James led a contingent of players who wore T-shirts that read "I Can't Breathe" during warm-ups, words uttered by Eric Garner when he was being choked to death by police.

NBA players have been thinking about race matters for years now. They have talked about it privately and spoken out publicly. They have made provocative gestures and

Draymond Green celebrates following Kevin Durant's steal and dunk during Team USA's gold medal victory against Serbia. (AP Images)

silent moves to promote change. And now they are about to represent the very country in which their presence, at minimum, solicits a passionate response.

Their plan as they head to Brazil? These 12 black men, ranging in age from 24 to 32, aim to be the change they want to see in the world.

"It's about a whole country that we're representing on the biggest stage that you could possibly be on," Carmelo Anthony said. "Using that platform to go out there and perform, I think the world seeing us, and our country seeing us, unite during this time, I think that's a message within itself."

Anthony, 32, is one of the most outspoken players. In April 2015, he marched with peaceful protesters in Baltimore outraged over the death of Freddie Gray, who died in police custody.

The elder statesmen on Team USA, Anthony's example and concern sets a tone for the rest of the team. The push these days is for involvement at the community level. Before their ESPY moment, Anthony took to Instagram to encourage his colleagues to demand change at the local level.

"You've got to respect and honor a person like that," DeMar DeRozan said of Anthony. "We stand by him 110 percent."

The imagery is powerful. One of the issues at the core of the issues between the police and African-American community is the perception of black men. The police involved in these incidents, and some around the country, responding out of fear, using deadly force under the assumption their lives are in danger. But protesters question the legitimacy of that fear and contend it is steeped in racism.

The victorious Team USA basketball squad poses with its gold medals after defeating Serbia 96-66. (AP Images)

But come the Olympics, these 12 African-American men won't represent anything to be afraid of, save for their smothering defense and transition offense. They plan to chip away at perceptions with their graciousness, attacking stigmas with their kindness and selflessness.

And, they hope, the positive image they display softens stereotypes and challenge Americans to follow their lead.

"It starts with each individual," Sacramento Kings center DeMarcus Cousins said. "How can we better ourselves on a daily basis? Every time it's a situation, we get to finger pointing. And don't get me wrong, it's a lot of messed up situations. But it starts with ourselves every day ... and then the rest will handle itself."

# DEFENSIVE STOPPER

## Klay Thompson Relishes Defensive Role on Team USA

By Marcus Thompson II | July 22, 2016

Klay Thompson hates Kyrie Irving. OK, maybe hate is a strong word.

"I dislike him," Thompson said with his trademark smirk. "But I respect him. I haven't forgotten what he did to us."

Thompson is joking of course. He and Irving have known each other, played against each other, for years. They came into the league together. But Thompson still has his feelings over the way Irving torched the Warriors in the NBA Finals. Specifically, torched Thompson, the Warriors' usual solution to the elite point guards.

Yeah, Thompson also missed key shots that could have propelled the Warriors to an NBA Finals win. But not being able to stop Irving stings more. And it's that spirit that explains why Thompson is a prized member of this Team USA edition.

Thompson's fanciest feature is his outside shot. He has the most textbook form in the NBA. When he's feeling it, the display is jaw-dropping. But on Team USA — which has natural scorers in Kevin Durant, Carmelo Anthony and Irving — Thompson is valuable even if his shot isn't falling. His 3-point shooting is bonus. The threat of it is enough as opponents sticking to Thompson creates space, which is in short supply in international play.

But he is also the guy the Americans can sick on opposing guards and make their lives miserable. That's a key piece in what coach Mike Krzyzewski is saying might be the best defensive team USA has ever fielded. He gave Argentina fits in the tuneup in Las Vegas, a 111-74 victory for Team USA. Manu Ginobili didn't score until Thompson left the game.

"Klay is really one of the great, complete players on this planet," Krzyzewski said. "He's more than a shooter. He's an outstanding offensive player who loves to

Klay Thompson pressures Team China guard Sui Ran during Team USA's 107-57 exhibition win at Oracle Arena.
(Doug Duran/Staff)

Klay Thompson defends Argentina guard and longtime San Antonio Spur Manu Ginobili during Team USA's 111-74 exhibition victory. (AP Images)

play defense and really never seems to get tired. He has a great motor. I loved him in the World Cup and I know I'm going to love him in Rio."

At 6-foot-7, Thompson is long enough to stay glued to quicker, smaller players. He is also 215 pounds, hardly skinny. He has a sturdy base that allows him to absorb contact and be physical with the player he's defending.

It takes an elite talent to give Thompson problems. And even then, it bothers him.

You know what else bothers him? Not making All-NBA Defense.

"It needs improvement, you think?" Thompson said of his defense. "I'm just kidding. I'm just seeing how I fit in on this team, whether it's spotting up from 3 or defending their best guard or whatever it is. Just trying to find my niche, find my role

and just go from there. Luckily for us, we have five, six days to figure it out."

Here is the part most don't know about Thompson: He's always prided himself on defense. When he was a sophomore in high school, UCLA coach Ben Howland told him he moved his feet well. That was almost like the head cheerleader telling him he was cute.

Then in a summer league game, Thompson matched up with Brandon Jennings, the best point guard in Los Angeles. Thompson walked away from that matchup not torched and feeling pretty good. He's been defending point guards ever since.

But his shooting prowess has always overlooked his defensive potential and production. Coming out of Washington State, Thompson was scouted as a poor defender. It wasn't until then-coach Mark Jackson started putting him on opposing point guards —

most notably Denver's Ty Lawson and San Antonio's Tony Parker in the 2013 playoffs — that Thompson began standing out as a defender.

Back then, Thompson struggled off the ball, which requires more focus than physical ability. But now, having been sharpened against the likes of Chris Paul and Russell Westbrook and, yes, Irving, Thompson is more than just a guy who can move his feet. He thwarts offensive game plans, wears down his opponent. And he's gotten better at team defense and holding his own against bigger players.

James Harden and LeBron James are the only players who give him problems regularly. Fortunately for Team USA, no one else in the world has perimeter players that good.

"He's an incredible defender," Irving said. "Think about it. He guards (three positions). He does whatever is asked of him every single night. Having a great guy like that, that also can bring an offensive threat. That's a complete player."

Klay Thompson fights Australia big man David Andersen for a rebound. Team USA won the hard-fought matchup 98-88.
(AP Images)

# A MEETING OF MEGASTARS

## First of Many Happy Moments for Kevin Durant, Warriors?

### By Tim Kawakami | July 26, 2016

Bob Myers was doing a routine interview, during a routine exhibition-game halftime, saying routine things, and then all of a sudden he didn't need to say anything.

The Warriors' general manager just had to point 20 feet away, at Kevin Durant racing over to embrace Stephen Curry.

And the two Warriors teammates — and league MVPs — beaming and giggling like kids.

What a thing.

"Stuff like that," Myers said, after a good and happy pause as the Oracle crowd roared at the sight of their MVPs, "is good to see.

"That's what makes it fun. Seeing guys that like playing basketball together. That's worth it right there."

Then Myers and I just let the scene soak in for a little bit, because it was a this-is-for-real moment, at least for me.

"Just catching up," Durant said after the game of his Curry chat.

"Good to see him. Glad he came to support us — him and 'Dre (Andre Iguodala)."

Curry was a late-arriving audience member for this Team USA-China pre-Olympics exhibition at Oracle, and Durant is the team's dominant scorer.

Curry is skipping these Olympics to heal up for the coming NBA season, and Durant just signed with the Warriors in one of the biggest free-agent acquisitions of all time.

Two different people. Two megastars. Joined in one orbit, for real, right there.

For this moment, in front of about 18,000 fans, with Iguodala sitting nearby, and Draymond Green and Klay Thompson also playing for Team USA, Curry and Durant were the merged personification of everything epic about this coming Warriors season.

In his debut game at Oracle Arena, Kevin Durant dunks over Team China center Wang Zhelin. (Doug Duran/Staff)

69

"Coming back here, obviously, it was a USA thing, but to me it's more about him (Durant) than anything," Green said after the game.

"For him to come here, his first game played here as a member of our team, in a Team USA jersey … nobody will look at it that way, but that was history."

Of course, Durant delivered early, as ordered up by Team USA point guard Kyrie Irving — who happened to make the shot in Game 7 that lifted Cleveland over the Warriors in the NBA Finals.

Green said Irving told Durant he was going to him right away, and that happened to be in the first eight seconds, off of the opening tip, and Durant took Irving's pass and immediately buried a 3-pointer.

To the great joy of the Oracle crowd and Durant's new teammates.

"It was amazing," Green said. "Came out guns blazing, which is good to see.

"Just to play with him on this floor is great. He was definitely excited."

Said Durant: "I knew I would pull the first shot — since yesterday."

Durant went on to score Team USA's first 10 points — and finished with 13 in the eventual 107-57 blowout.

But, of course, this wasn't about the score or even actually about Team USA rounding into Olympic form, since a gold medal in Rio is fairly inevitable.

As Green noted, this was about Durant coming to Oakland as a Warrior for the first time, and for everybody in the building to fully understand that this is for real now.

Maybe even Durant felt it, at least as far as Green could see and hear.

"He was himself in the locker room (before the game)," Green said of Durant. "He kept saying, 'Man, I got the jitters, like first-game-type jitters.' But it was great to see."

Coach Mike Krzyzewski purposely started all three Warriors in this game as a nod to the home crowd, and Green took the microphone at the start to thank the fans, with Thompson and Durant alongside. Iguodala was courtside with his son, and Myers was nearby.

Then Curry made a dramatic, crowd-rousing entrance during the second quarter.

"Make sure you all give Steph some crap for his grand entrance," Green said with a laugh.

Didn't matter — Durant bolted out of the locker room at halftime straight to Curry's courtside seat, and that's when the embrace took place.

If you were there, you probably won't forget it.

"It's fun to see him out there knowing he's going to be playing for us, to be honest," Myers said. "Selfishly, it's fun to see.

"It's good to see Andre and Steph out here supporting them."

And Durant looked pretty happy, didn't he Bob?

"You could see … but, you know, he hasn't had that moment yet," Myers said. "I think it was a precursor — an appetizer, I should say."

A pretty good Warriors moment. A loud one. And just the first one. 🏀

Kevin Durant, one of three Warriors to start in front of the home crowd at Oracle Arena, handles the ball during the 107-57 blowout victory against China. (Doug Duran/Staff)

# COACH'S APPROVAL

## Steve Kerr Likes What He Sees with Kevin Durant and Company

By Marcus Thompson II | July 25, 2016

Steve Kerr said it probably won't hit him until training camp, when Kevin Durant is wearing a Warriors jersey.

But Tuesday night, the Warriors head coach, along with the rest of the Bay Area, will get his first up-close look at the coming reality. Team USA, featuring three of his Warriors stars, takes on China at Oracle Arena on its exhibition tour heading to the Olympics in Rio.

Kerr has only watched his guys — Durant, Klay Thompson and Draymond Green — playing together on television thus far and is forced to temper his excitement over the possibilities.

"They look great," Kerr said in a phone interview. "Not surprising, because none of them dominate the ball. All of them move the ball. One of the things that made (Durant) so attractive to us is that it didn't feel like it would be difficult to blend in."

Durant was booed in Los Angeles on Sunday. But he is sure to be serenaded at Oracle, a preface to the love he will receive when finally wearing blue and gold. Especially the way Durant and Thompson have clicked together, finding each other and serving as Team USA's resident gunners, there are sure to be some glimpses of the Warriors' future.

Kerr said this experience is good for the Warriors trio. A minicamp preparing them for training camp.

"It helps," Kerr said. "I'm happy that they're spending the next few weeks together. Not only playing together but getting to know each other. All that stuff matters."

The Warriors' offense will certainly have more layers to it. Adding a talent such as Durant to the core — replacing a career 10.1 points per game scorer, Harrison Barnes, with Durant's 27.4 average — takes the offense to a new level.

But Kerr maintains nothing will change foundationally. The Warriors will still "move the ball like crazy and run," as Kerr put it, and they now have two players capable of creating offense in Durant and Stephen Curry. So the biggest adjustment might be feel and comfort.

The Warriors' three existing All-Stars have four years together under their belt. They know each other's strengths and weaknesses, likes and dislikes. Curry can sense when Thompson is feeling it. Green knows the best angles to set Curry screens. Thompson knows how to make himself visible to Curry in transition. Those things come with time together.

That's what the Warriors are getting to learn with Durant, an education on each other's games.

"We don't have to change a whole lot of stuff," Kerr said. "We'll probably plug Kevin into what we already do. ... We can definitely add some things. Kevin makes any offense look better than it actually is. It's still about players sharing the ball. Playing with pace. Playing unselfishly."

Kerr said the Warriors will definitely use their status as villains, mostly as comic relief. Knowing Kerr, he's lining up Gary Oldman to address the team about playing the villain role. Ron Adams is being suited for a Darth Vader costume to wear during film sessions.

The light moments will be needed. The Warriors have a hard road ahead. The pressure will be immense. The vitriol thrown their way will be hectic. They will

need to adjust quickly. Team USA is giving them a head start.

"It's going to require some work together, and we're going to have to go through it to feel it," Kerr said. "It won't be easy all the time, that's for sure. This is what they all wanted. We're going to have a lot of pressure on us. That's fine. We welcome that."

Warriors head coach Steve Kerr has reason to smile, as he welcomes star Kevin Durant onto what was already one of the NBA's great teams. (Dan Honda/Staff)

# RED, WHITE, AND GREEN

## Draymond Green Brings Exceptional Skill to Team USA

By Marcus Thompson II | August 2, 2016

Draymond Green thought his Olympic career was done. Before his senior season at Michigan State, he represented America in the 2011 World University Games in China. When he took off that No. 10 jersey five years ago this month, after they edged Germany in the fifth-place game, Green was sure it was the last time he'd wear USA on his chest.

Since then, the NBA has changed. The evolution has Green in Brazil for the 2016 Summer Games.

The change? The world's best league began to emphasize skill. And with the NBA feeding USA Basketball, that means Team USA has become a beacon of basketball skill.

There was a time when the international game was reputed for skill. America's dominance was based on athleticism, size and depth. Eventually, the skill of the world caught up with the athleticism and the USA had to adjust.

The 2016 edition is now elite because of its skill. The pedigree and IQ of this roster is excellent up and down the roster. Centers can handle the ball. Forwards can play point. Everyone can pass and defend in a unit.

America heads into these games flaunting the kind of skill that can outclass any other nation.

By the way, USA is still the deepest. Still the biggest up and down the roster. Still the most athletic — just Google "DeMar DeRozan" and "360 miss" to see the evidence. But at every position, the Americans will have an advantage in hoop sophistication.

The Warriors, taking their cue from the San Antonio Spurs, have been major players in this new reality. What is known around the league as small ball is really skill ball.

Draymond Green, who can deftly defend all five positions, goes against France's Boris Diaw, an NBA veteran, in the 2016 Olympics. (AP Images)

The Warriors, evolving on the style of play Don Nelson popularized, sacrifice size for skill and won 140 regular season games over the past two seasons and were oh-so-close to back-to-back championships.

The Warriors lost the 2016 NBA Finals in part because Cleveland shortened its rotation to its most skilled players and outdueled the defending champions.

Now, the Warriors and Cavaliers being the class of the league have ignited the league-wide trend of valuing players who have the skills to play multiple positions and produce in a variety of ways. And that trend is evident on Team USA.

So it's fitting that three players — Green, Klay Thompson and former Warriors forward Harrison Barnes — who helped change the tide of the league made the 12-man roster. Stephen Curry would have assuredly made it if he weren't injured, so it could have been four.

Cleveland would have had two players if LeBron James opted to play. But point guard Kyrie Irving, who was pivotal in upsetting the Warriors, gives Team USA a floor general who can pass, penetrate and make shots at an elite level.

And the best player on Team USA is Kevin Durant, now with the Warriors. He's in essence a 6-foot-11 guard. He can handle, penetrate, shoot, rebound and protect the rim. DeMarcus Cousins, the Sacramento Kings' center, is a giant in the paint with footwork unbecoming of someone his size to go with a decent jumper and the ability to handle the ball.

The chances of America upset by a team with sound fundamentals has dramatically decreased. Even the few international teams loaded with NBA talent, who have the benefit of playing together for years, will have their hands full contending with America's versatility.

Spain will be the toughest foe but suffered a big blow when Marc Gasol was ruled out. They still have NBA starters in Pau Gasol, Ricky Rubio and Nikolai Mirotic — and former NBA players in Rudy Fernandez, Sergio Rodriguez and Juan Carlos Navarro.

Lithuania and Argentina, ranked No. 3 and 4 by FIBA, can be a problem in a perfect storm. France, ranked 5th, has a mix of young and veteran talent that can be dangerous. Tony Parker, Boris Diaw, Nicolas Batum, Rudy Gobert — the French has some NBA talent.

But they all pale in comparison to USA. The Americans won't have to impose their will physically to win. They can also play the free-flowing, fundamental game that used to give our country problems. USA has caught and passed the rest of the world in the skill department. And the globe can thank the Warriors for helping. 🏀

Thinking he had played his last game for an American team in international play during the 2011 World University Games, Draymond Green took great pride in winning a gold medal during the 2016 Olympics. (AP Images)

# JUST KD BEING KD

## Durant Provides Energy Boost for Team USA

By Mark Purdy | August 17, 2016

Now that was more like it.

The USA men's basketball team finally found its identity in Rio. After scuffling around way more than necessary during preliminary rounds of the Olympic tournament, the good old Estados Unidos showed up for its quarterfinal elimination game against Argentina and found the answer it was seeking.

Warriors fans will like the answer.

Kevin Durant, not so shockingly, has turned out to be the USA's basketball centerpiece of these Games. The newest Golden State Dub has become the American drubber. He drubs into submission any opponent who tries to stop him.

Durant did not just score 27 points in a 105-78 dismantling of an opponent that has frequently vexed the USA in international play. Durant more or less mesmerized both the Argentina players and their thousands of singing and screaming fans inside Carioca Arena 1. He scored 13 of the USA's first 19 points and set the killer defensive tone as the rout gradually kicked into gear.

"The only thing we really changed today," Durant said, referencing earlier close calls to France and Serbia, "was our passion and energy. We locked in on that. And we fed off not playing better the last few games."

Kyrie Irving, the USA point guard, was expecting Durant to do exactly what he did.

"He was just being himself," Irving said. "This is the stage he thrives on. We can count on KD being KD in the biggest moments, which we've all kind of come to respect and rely on."

With Durant as the USA's leading scorer in this tournament (18.5 points per game) and leading defensive rebounder (4.6 per game) and second leading assist man (3.9 per game, second only to Irving)

Kevin Durant pointed the way for Team USA against Argentina, scoring 13 of his squad's first 19 points during the victory. (AP Images)

and leading minutes-played man (28:16 per game) ... well, I think we can all see what the game plan will be as the USA moves on to the semifinals on Friday against Spain. The other semifinal matches Australia and Serbia. Friday's winners meet Sunday for the gold medal.

The American roster obviously contains a wealth of talent. Irving is a trigger. Paul George kicked the team into a more intense gear when he entered Wednesday's game and created havoc. Carmelo Anthony fills up the basket.

But so far over six games, the one USA player that opposing teams have been unable to stop here — at the moments when a stop is most needed — is the man wearing the red, white and blue No. 5 jersey here in Brazil. He has been a nightmare matchup.

Needless to say, this bodes well for the winter of 2016-17 at Oracle Arena.

Consider: If a man's performance can cause an entire South American nation to have a nervous basketball breakdown, then surely that same man will create many problems on a Tuesday night in November against the Clippers. I believe basketball scholars refer to this principle as Kobe's First Law Of Transitory Supremacy.

I was hardly expecting Durant to fall on his face here. With LeBron James and Stephen Curry choosing to sit out this tournament for various reasons, Durant was certainly among

Kevin Durant, who led all scorers with 27 points, shoots during the 105-78 victory against Argentina. (AP Images)

the best four or five players on the USA roster. But with so many other big names and personalities surrounding him, it has been interesting to see how Durant has elevated himself to the very top of the very top.

Even more interesting, as we Bay Area types get to learn more about the guy, is how Durant has accomplished that feat mentally. He opened the door to that a bit after Wednesday's game.

"I was telling myself this morning that I am at my best when I don't care about the result," Durant said. "That may be different for other players. But for me, I'm way more free and more aggressive and the game is more fun for me if I don't care about the outcome. I know if I just go out there and be who I am, the outcome will dictate itself. I just try to play and be free."

Sounds sort of zen, doesn't it? And actually rather amazing. So. One of the world's best players plays his best when he does not care about the outcome? All right. Intriguing. But in the real NBA world, as in the real Olympic world, results and outcomes do matter.

Durant cares about those outcomes, too. He must. Otherwise, he wouldn't win so much. And on another level, every follower of the Warriors is crazy-curious to see the result of how he will fit into the team's lineup and rotation.

So far, there are practically no clues about that here. The other two Yankee Doodle Dubs on the USA roster, Klay Thompson and Draymond Green, continue to play largely

supportive roles here. The three of them are almost never on the court together.

Thompson, of course, had his breakout 30-point game the other day against France. But otherwise, he has been a quiet purr on the USA soundtrack while averaging 18:44 of playing time. Thompson had four points Wednesday. Like his USA teammates, he has often been admiring Durant and feeding him while giving up shot opportunities. Will it be the same come November and December?

Meanwhile, Green is getting even less playing time per game (11:25) from USA coach Mike Krzyzewski but is bringing energy off the bench. Green definitely made himself known Wednesday in the USA's second period when they outscored Argentina by 20 points.

But with two more games to reach the gold medal podium, there's no question which of the Doodle Dubs is the most crucial piece. It's cool to see Durant embrace the role. That's another thing we have learned about him over the past two weeks. He's quite patriotic.

"At the end of the game today," Durant said, "you could hear the Argentina fans were yelling so loud in here and it was great. But then right behind them, there were our fans yelling, 'U-S-A, U-S-A, U-S-A.' It gave me chills."

The mission of conquering the rest of the world gives Durant chills. Durant gives the rest of the world major problems. Warriors fans are especially going to enjoy that formula. 🏀

# GOLDEN BOY

## Durant gives Warriors Fans a Preview of What's to Come

By Mark Purdy | August 21, 2016

Kevin Durant dismantled Serbia here in less time than it takes to order a caipirinha, the national cocktail of Brazil. He also applied a quicker knockout blow.

In the gold medal game for Team USA, the newest Golden State Warrior was instrumental in the Americans' pull-away stretch that turned a somewhat close game into a rout.

Durant scored eight consecutive points in one second-quarter stretch and rang up 24 in the first half as his team used a 33-14 run to take a 52-29 halftime lead. From there, the U.S. coasted to a 96-66 victory. Durant finished with 30 points. He didn't even play in the fourth quarter and was as happy as anyone afterward.

"It's my second gold medal," said Durant, who was also on the London 2012 team, "and the feeling stays the same. It never gets old."

The Carioca Arena complex is thousands of miles away from the Bay Area. But no question, Durant's move to Northern California was a subtext to all he did here as an Olympian. The topic came up almost every day, in almost every interview session. Jerry Colangelo, the NBA executive who also serves as managing director for USA Basketball, even felt compelled to address it after Durant's performance.

"He's gone through a lot of examination with the fact that he signed with the Warriors," Colangelo said. "He's been under a little bit of pressure. And to see him bust out like he did here was wonderful. I think it's really going to help his psyche moving forward. I couldn't be happier for him."

If there was extra pressure on Durant to be a star-spangled bell cow — which he was, averaging 19.4 points over eight games and finishing as the team's leading defensive

Durant dunks home two of his 30 points during Team USA's gold medal victory. (AP Images)

rebounder — it barely showed. Yet after some of the early round-robin games when the U.S. speed-bumped its way through four victories by 10 points or fewer, Durant was bummed. Mike Krzyzewski, coaching his third and final Olympics, could sense that and intervened.

"I wasn't being myself," Durant said. "Coach sat me down and showed me some film of 2012. He said, 'I want to see that guy again.' He just told me to be me. I was trying too hard to sacrifice and make that extra pass, and I was taken away from my game. I guess I just woke up. When I'm smiling out there, screaming and beating my chest, showing emotion, that's when I'm really lost in the game. I got away from that."

Serbia, which lost by three points to the U.S. during the preliminary, wishes that Durant had stayed away. There was no doubt that when he wanted to be, he was the best player on the floor, even with all the talent on the U.S. roster.

Stefan Markovic, probably Serbia's best player, hinted that his team knew what was coming and might have been intimidated.

"You can't wait to attack," Markovic said. "They are all superstars. If you let them play, they will kill you."

Fortunately, no murder was committed, before or after the medal ceremony. But that ceremony, during which all 12 players put their hands over their hearts for the national anthem, brought out visible emotion in many of the players. That included all three of the Warriors here — Durant, Klay Thompson and Draymond Green.

Thompson also played a strong role in the victory, scoring 12 points and lobbing one memorable assist to Los Angeles Clippers center DeAndre Jordan that resulted in an exclamation-point dunk early in the second half.

"Everyone knew what was at stake today," Thompson said. "We only beat these guys by three last time. We just raised the level of intensity."

The Warriors' own Mr. Intensity, meanwhile, continued to play a lesser role in the U.S. game plan. Green didn't enter the game until the fourth quarter. The Olympic tournament is such a one-off event, it might or might not mean something important that Krzyzewski gave Green light minutes during the entire tournament.

Basically, for whatever reason, Coach K declined to ever utilize a small lineup that might mimic the Warriors' offensive template. Instead, DeMarcus Cousins was more frequently on the floor, using his big body.

Green would not go there when asked if any of this bothered him. Of all the Yankee Doodle Dubs, he actually seemed the most blissful about his Olympic experience.

"I came here thinking, I'm going to do whatever I can and do whatever I have to do," Green said. "If that means play a lot, if that means not play a lot, that's the way it is. The goal is to win a gold medal. And I reached that goal. To do this on behalf of your country, I'm blessed to have this opportunity."

Some unforgettable moments of his time here, Green said, were away from the basketball venue. He was able to attend other Olympic events such as Michael Phelps' races and the Saturday night gold medal men's soccer game won by Brazil. It capped off the entire journey.

"It's a little more than you thought," Green said. "It's one of those things where you go in with such high expectations, and you're like, 'Aww, I hope it reaches the expectations that I have — and it completely blows it out of the water. Man, I'm thrilled. It's one of your lifelong dreams, one you think you're never going to get. And to be here, it's amazing."

Thompson had said that he would be just as proud of his Olympic gold medal as his NBA championship because the achievements are equal. He wasn't backing down from that view.

"It's the same," Thompson said. "This lasts a lifetime. I'm proud of every individual on this team. It was worth every minute of sacrifice during our offseason. Not a lot of people can say they're Olympians, let alone gold medalists."

Of course, some gold medalists are always more equal than others. So this will most certainly be remembered as the Games Of Durant. His exploits here in Rio gave followers of the Warriors no reason to do anything but be eager for what he might accomplish at Oracle Arena this winter. Maybe the club level bar will salute him by serving caipirinhas. 🏀

After Team USA defeated Serbia 96-66, Warriors star Kevin Durant celebrates the victory, which represents his second Olympic gold medal. (AP Images)

# CAMP WARRIORS

## Where Steph Curry Might Just Deliver You Pizza

### By Courtney Cronin | August 16, 2016

The voice sounded vaguely like Stephen Curry's, but the subject matter was certainly odd.

"I've got Dominos Pizza!"

There at Brigham Young University's satellite campus in Laie, Hawaii, 12-year-old Bay Area native Astrid Vallar couldn't believe her eyes as she and her roommates opened their dorm room door.

There indeed stood the NBA's reigning two-time MVP, posing as a pizza delivery man.

"I froze," Vallar said. "He came and surprised a bunch of us the first night. We freaked out."

At some basketball camps hosted by an NBA player, participants are lucky to walk away with an autograph. At Curry's overnight Warriors Basketball Camp, campers get surprise visits from the Golden State star and invaluable instruction from Curry himself on how to master the drills that have made him a sensation.

It's possible that the next Curry-in-the-making may have been at that camp in Hawaii or walking around the halls of the Warriors practice facility in Oakland.

He or she could have also been spotted shooting with their non-dominant hand, working on helpside defense or trying to master moving without the ball at one of 23 Warriors Basketball Camps held in 15 Bay Area cities and two outside the region.

More than 3,800 kids age 7 to 16 participated in this series of day and overnight camps this summer. Within weeks of opening enrollment in January, all 23 camps sold out for the first time in their 17-year history. That was long before Golden State achieved its own monumental success with 73 wins in the 2015-16 season.

Shortly after signing with the team, Warriors center Zaza Pachulia high-fives a basketball camper at Golden State's practice facility. (Aric Crabb/Staff)

After a two-month stretch, this week marks the final session of the summer held at Kaiser Permanente Arena in Santa Cruz.

These camps have become the place for youths to learn the fundamentals of the game while getting a closer look at the Warriors organization.

For an entire week of instruction, camp cost $425 for sessions at the practice facility and $395 for other sites in the Bay Area. Draymond Green's overnight camp in Seaside was $1,100 from June 24-27 while Curry's session totaled $2,250. Warriors Basketball Camps also routinely offer scholarships for campers to attend.

The practice courts where Curry works on his jumpshot while Klay Thompson perfects his crossover move is one of several spots the instruction takes place. Few other camps allow youths to learn about the game on the floor where a championship team was built. Even fewer can boast about actually helping launch an NBA career.

\* \* \*

At the start of each session, campers get to pick out their jersey. Curry's No. 30 is always in popular demand along with 23 (Green), 11 (Klay Thompson), and even 40 (the departed Harrion Barnes).

Vallar proudly sports No. 9 in honor of her favorite Warrior, Andre Iguodala. In a few months she'll try out for her middle school basketball team, hoping to display the skills she learned at the three camps she attended at the practice facility along with both Curry and Green's overnight sessions.

In a few years she, too, could be someone's favorite player and the next success story spawned from these camps.

"I feel like every year I've come here I've gotten better," Vallar said. "My weak side is my right side and they taught me how to do a lot of stuff with that side that I wasn't able to before."

Oakland native Will Cherry, who made his NBA debut during the 2014-15 season with the Cleveland Cavaliers, once walked that same path as Vallar, learning the fundamentals of the game at Warriors Basketball Camps.

Golden State may also deserve some credit for discovering the potential in Miami Heat point guard Tyler Johnson, who is the top product of these camps.

Johnson attended Warriors Basketball Camp as a preteen before starring at St. Francis High in Mountain View and later Fresno State. This summer as a free agent, Johnson inked a four-year, $50 million contract extension with Miami.

A decade before making his 2015 NBA debut with the Heat in front of his home crowd at Oracle Arena, it was the Warriors that Johnson sought out for assistance in taking his game to the next level.

*Dear Warriors,*

*My name is Tyler Johnson*

*I'm from Mt. View, California. I am writing to see if maybe I could get a scholarship to you (sic) Warrior Camp. I am an athlete and my parents don't have a lot of extra money to spend to send us to camps, so I think that the Warrior Camp will improve my game.*

"It just blows us away," Golden State Warriors senior director of youth basketball Jeff Addiego said. "Feels good that we had campers who went all the way and took this

# Few other camps allow youths to learn about the game on the floor where a championship team was built. Even fewer can boast about actually helping launch an NBA career.

to the highest level. We can't wait to hear about the next camper to do the same thing."

\* \* \*

Many of the 100-plus coaches that help out at Warriors Basketball Camps throughout the year are former campers who played at all levels, from junior college to professional ball.

"You can't just have All-Americans or professional players and have that be the base of our staff," Addiego said. "It's great for us to have a mix of good teachers."

For parents, the type of instruction their kids receive and who it's coming from positively foreshadows some of their own hopes for their children.

"These are top-notch coaches," said Florence Woo, whose 8-year-old son Rykan attended two weeks of WBC at the practice facility in July. "To be able to get coaches of this caliber who really enjoy teaching and some of them who were actual campers themselves when they were 8 or 10 years old is special. To see them go through that journey and come back as a coach is great to see as a parent."

And it wouldn't be a Warriors Basketball Camp without getting the big hitters in the organization involved.

When Addiego approached Green about hosting his own overnight camp at CSU Monterey Bay at the end of June, the energetic forward was all in.

"We had 10 different groups at that camp and he spent time playing one-on-one with each group," Addiego said. "When he was done with that he was in a full sweat. He took a very hands-on approach."

There in front of hundreds of campers, Green spoke about his journey to the NBA, offering advice and inspiration to the eager ears.

"There was this one speech that Draymond gave us that was really, really good," Vallar said. "He was motivating us that we can't stop in the middle. If we want to reach our best, we can't stop when we're tired and rest. We have to keep going."

Golden State general manager Bob Myers and forward Kevon Looney popped into sessions in Walnut Creek and Oakland. Green, Ian Clark and rookie Damian Jones also made surprise appearances this summer.

An hour after Warriors center ZaZa Pachulia signed a one-year contract in July, the first group he spoke to outside of the media was over 150 campers at the Warriors practice facility. One by one campers lined up to get their picture with the Georgian center and an autograph.

It was one of the many perks for Woo's son, who may have a new favorite player.

"How cool was that? (Pachulia) took the time to actually engage with all of the children," Woo said. "Where else would

(Rykan) get to see that? It's an opportunity for him to say he saw him in the beginning and now he'll be able to watch him later on knowing he got to meet the newest player on the Warriors."

\* \* \*

While centered in the Bay Area, Warriors Basketball Camps have a worldwide draw. This summer alone, youths from Spain, Shanghai and Beijing traveled to the United States to participate in the week-long sessions. Curry's Hawaii camp had kids from California, Wisconsin, West Virginia, Pennsylvania, New York, Texas and Florida.

Woo, a San Francisco native who now lives in Lake Forest, Illinois, wanted to give her son a "world-class experience" this summer and flew him out for two weeks of camp run by his favorite team.

What she noticed upon the first day was the level of instruction Rykan received was exponentially different than other camps he had attended.

"They were out there doing drills I did in high school," Woo said. "The fact that they're teaching them these skills at such an early age and pushing the kids, it's not just the standard 'day care' that you might get at some of these other basketball camps."

Rykan Woo and his cousin, Micah Chan, who also attended WBC, left camp each day inspired to put more time into their game.

"We're driving every day from San Francisco across the Bay Bridge to Oakland and back, and the two of them just talk non-stop about what they've learned and what they did that day," Woo said. "Even after the clock stops at 3, they're asking if they can go outside and practice some of the skills they learned earlier in the day."

Curry's famed two-ball drill that displays incredible hand-eye coordination along with ball handling, timing and passing is among the instruction for campers throughout all of summer sessions. At the overnight session in Hawaii, campers got a first-hand look at how to master the drill from No. 30 himself.

Curry brought up Chris Head to demonstrate the dribbling exercise. Head is yet another success story from Warriors Basketball Camp.

The camper-turned-Hampton University-standout-turned counselor caught Curry's eye four years ago when he began his overnight sessions. The Golden State point guard began using Head as a body double for the two-ball drill and has assisted Curry with several workouts over the last year.

As Curry instructed, Head mimicked his actions. He dribbled a ball in his left hand while the one in his right went around the front of his leg before he caught it in the back – Curry's "in-and-out" drill. As he picked up speed, Head crossed the ball in front of him, dribbled through his legs and then behind him before passing the ball back.

Not once did Head bobble the ball or mess up, drawing the highest praise in the gym and serving as an example of practice paying off.

"Chris would be the first to tell you four years ago he couldn't have done that," Curry told campers. "He would have been okay, he would have lost the ball a couple of times. He might have got a little bit frustrated, a little bit down on himself, but he kept working. And now, that was pretty flawless. That might have been better than I do."

James Michael McAdoo poses for pictures with the Santa Cruz Warriors basketball campers at Kaiser Permanente Arena.
(Dan Coyro/Staff)

# WARRIORS
# IN DEPTH

# GENERATION STEPH

## Curry is the Greatest Show of Our Time

By Tim Kawakami | December 4, 2015

The Stephen Curry Revolution is happening every game, but not just in arenas and not measured only by the NBA standings or record book.

This is a night-by-night, worldwide sports epiphany, witnessed by everybody great or small who can't resist tuning into the greatest show of our time.

"To me, my hero, other than Michael Jordan, growing up was Isiah Thomas," said two-time NBA MVP Steve Nash.

"But in some ways, I wish I was a 13-year-old starting to play basketball for the first time so I could grow up watching (Curry) play and emulating him. That'd be pretty powerful.

"You know, I hope my (6-year-old) son likes basketball."

That's the unique power of what Curry is doing these days with the 20-0 Warriors — it's far beyond his team affiliation or the normal demographics of this sport.

He's NBA Elvis. Today's Jesse Owens. He's the new thing that blows away all existing limits and boundaries.

So yes, the victories are important. Last season's championship and Curry's MVP award were crowning milestones, no doubt.

And Curry's poise and grace throughout it all — his connection to his teammates, coaches and fans — serve as the largest exclamation points to his ascension.

But as a cultural barometer, the specific Curry Moments — most recently, his incredible 28-point, third-quarter performance in Charlotte — are essentially stand-alone landmarks.

We watch. He plays. The night turns electric.

Brent Barry, a 14-year NBA veteran and now a national TV analyst, says his 9-year-old

Steph Curry celebrates the Warriors win over the Oklahoma City Thunder in Game 7 of the 2016 NBA Western Conference finals. (Aric Crabb/Staff)

95

son asks him one thing every afternoon: "Is Steph playing tonight?" And against Charlotte they were another witness for Curry.

"He won't miss games," Barry said of his son, "just like Steph won't miss shots."

The NBA, of course, is not lacking for immense, compelling talents — starting with LeBron James and continuing through Kevin Durant, Tim Duncan, Russell Westbrook, Draymond Green and James Harden, among others.

But there is something different about Curry right now, in his prime (27, in his seventh NBA season) and accelerating his game well past even last season's MVP dominance.

As future Hall of Famer Kevin Garnett suggested recently, Curry is treading upon sacred NBA territory — where only Michael Jordan recently has tread.

With Curry and the Warriors at the forefront, lethal long-distance shooting has become basketball's most potent force, and Curry proves it every game. "Like Michael Jordan was a whole other thing, this guy is his own thing," Garnett told reporters. "It's beautiful for basketball."

Curry, who scored 40 points in only 30 minutes against Charlotte, now has six games of 40 points or more this season. The last player to do that in his team's first 20 games: Jordan in 1986.

But this is not close to the same thing, because Jordan and Curry represent different levels of NBA invincibility.

Curry poses with his back-to-back MVP trophies at Oracle Arena. In 2016, Curry was the first player in NBA history to be unanimously voted MVP. (Jane Tyska/Staff)

In his prime, Jordan attacked the rim and defied gravity; Curry seems to exist in a dimension without it.

He just calmly places himself and the basketball wherever he wants while all other players whirl and tumble haphazardly around him.

NBA legend Jerry West, a Warriors executive, said the most notable part of Curry's career track is that he works so hard in the offseason and keeps taking enormous strides.

"I think he's going to create a new kind of player, to be honest with you," West said. "I think before it's all said and done, here's a guy that's going to make his own place in history in a completely different manner than these other players have done."

In just the past two seasons, Curry, who is right-handed, has developed such a great touch driving and shooting with his left hand that West says he sometimes teases Curry that he probably can't actually use his right hand.

With the possible exception of Pete Maravich's star-crossed career, the sport has never had such a pure shooter who can also weave through defenders to finish or flick the ball to open teammates.

And Curry is doing it better and certainly more consistently than Maravich ever did.

This isn't just about numbers, but the numbers are stunning: Curry made eight three-pointers against Charlotte, giving him 102 for the season — more than Larry Bird ever made in one season — in only 20 games.

Curry is averaging more than five three-point baskets per game, putting him on pace to destroy the regular-season record for threes (286), which he set last season.

Curry leads the league in scoring, plus-minus, true shooting percentage, PER ... and you don't have to know what all those stats mean except that this is a season for the ages and a career that will end up next to the immortals.

"I wouldn't compare him to Michael Jordan," said Nash, who retired last season and now serves as a consultant to the Warriors. "But I would say Steph is turning into a historical category of his own, in a way.

"He's in the prime of his career and will be for a few years, and the way he's improving and the level he's playing at is ... I think he's unlike anyone else. His ability to make shots and still handle the play-making duties is historic.

"I think you'd be hard-pressed to find a player more skilled than him in the history of the game."

Yes, Curry's teammates realize they're playing alongside somebody who is creating history every game.

Even more, they understand that Curry is the perfect person to do this and handle it all — for example, Curry only started shooting this often when he realized it was the best thing for the team.

"It's self-evident," said Warriors forward Andre Iguodala. "He's just in his ... kind of his own world.

"Things are good when you are who you think you are. And he is that. He's starting to know, 'That's who I am.' And when you're

Steph Curry is known for his long-range marksmanship but is equally adept at finding creative ways to get to the basket. (Aric Crabb/Staff)

playing with that much confidence, you have that talent and you work that hard, it's going to happen for you."

So has Curry changed the game?

"Yeah, for good and for bad," Iguodala said, possibly envisioning a future in which everyone is firing up shots outside their range.

Curry's game is definitely not difficult to embrace or to try to copy — everybody can shoot or dribble a ball.

"It seems to be a lot more accessible to the average fan or the hoop head or the gym rat," Barry said of Curry's game. "It isn't Steph jumping over two people on a fast break and hammering home dunks. It isn't a physical domination on the post."

You can imagine the result: Just as Jordan's career produced thousands of players trying to dunk every time they touched the ball, Curry's highlight reel could create legions of three-point shooters who can't actually shoot.

Recreation leagues, AAU games, college games and even the NBA might be full of long-heave chaos for a while, starring multitudes of Curry wannabes who can't and shouldn't try to be Curry.

But, as Nash suggests, if you look at the beauty and complexity of Curry's game, maybe that wouldn't be so bad.

It's an evolution, and Curry is the latest Big Bang.

"The game's evolving ... and it's a beautiful thing because it's about skill and dedication, commitment and inspiring a whole generation," Nash said.

"It's awesome to see. And I think it'll be fascinating to see what the next evolution will be because of Steph."

Nobody knows what that will be, nobody knows when that will happen.

What we know is that Curry, right here and now, is the greatest sports happening of this generation and one of the most important of all generations. 🏀

Above: Curry overcame ankle injuries early in his career to become one of the transcendent talents in recent NBA history. (Nhat V. Meyer/Staff) Opposite: A cool and calm personality off the court, Curry shows plenty of fire when he plays and has developed into a team leader. (Jose Carlos Fajardo/Staff)

# TEAM-FIRST TONE

## Klay Thompson Happy to Let Other Warriors Get the Attention

By Marcus Thompson II | February 13, 2016

The interview was delayed by an equipment hiccup. With Klay Thompson's media schedule packed and every minute accounted for, the NBA rep barked at the cameraman that his time would be cut short. He barked back about not starting his clock.

Meanwhile, Thompson picked up a basketball on the set. He started dribbling, working on his crossover against an imaginary defender. Every few seconds, he would rise up and shoot, the thump of the ball off the wall filling the meeting room. Unfazed by the inconvenience. Untouched by the minor tension.

It was a perfect picture of Thompson, the Warriors' two-time All-Star guard. Unfazed to the point he seems aloof. Unconcerned to the extent of appearing indifferent.

"That was always Klay's personality," said Indiana Pacers forward Paul George, who played AAU ball with Thompson. "He comes in, gets his work done. He doesn't need praise and glory. You just know what you're going to get from him. That's what you love about Klay."

This is one of the secret weapons of the Warriors' chemistry: Thompson's personality.

How does Stephen Curry flourish into one of the biggest stars on the planet without it producing envy in the Warriors' ranks? Same with Draymond Green's meteoric rise.

A big reason is Thompson. The Warriors' low-maintenance star, a gym rat still breaking in his superstar sneakers, sets a tone for the Warriors that serves as an invisible fertilizer.

Once part of a rising duo dubbed the Splash Brothers, Thompson is now

Klay Thompson had a terrific 2015-2016 season for the Warriors, averaging 22.1 points, 3.8 rebounds, and 2.1 assists per game, while shooting 42.5 percent from 3-point range. (Nhat V. Meyer/Staff)

undeniably the Kelly Rowland to Curry's Beyoncé.

Green, making his first All-Star appearance, has surpassed Thompson in status and recognition. Green's big personality and ever-improving game are

turning him into a coveted pitchman, getting deals with Beats by Dre and Foot Locker.

And this is happening while Thompson is on pace for career highs in field goal percentage and 3-pointers made, while back to defending point guards more often.

Yet Thompson doesn't care about that. At all.

"Why would I be mad at my teammates' success?" Thompson said, dismissing the premise. "First off, I can't do what Steph can do. Plus, I wouldn't be where I am without Steph, without Draymond, without my teammates. It's all about the team. Their success is my success."

This is much less a conscious effort by Thompson than a way of life. The flame doesn't attract this moth as it does most others. He's just getting comfortable in this position as an NBA star. He probably still doesn't fully grasp his status and the spoils that could come with it.

His demeanor gives Curry an invitation to be unabashed, which matters for a guy who dealt with tension from his last backcourt mate.

Thompson's nonchalance is a license for Green to be himself without having to navigate Thompson's feelings.

His focus on the team helps foster an unwritten code that prevents the bickering and beef from taking over the locker room.

"He has a good enough sense of humor to joke around," Green said, "But he stays in his lane and does his thing. Sometimes,

Above: Thompson rarely shows much emotion on the court, making the moments he does that much more notable. (Nhat V. Meyer/Staff) Opposite: Thompson is one of the best long-distance shooters in NBA history, including a career-high 276 threes made in 2015-2016 and the title in the 2016 Foot Locker Three-Point Contest at NBA All-Star Weekend. (Jose Carlos Fajardo/Staff)

Klay Thompson drives past the Oklahoma City Thunder's Andre Roberson in Game 4 of the 2016 NBA Western Conference finals. (Nhat V. Meyer/Staff)

especially now that more people may say something about me, it may seem like it's taking away from him. But Klay doesn't care. None of us do. That's why we're as good as we are. So it makes a huge difference that Klay is that way."

When Thompson was notified he made the All-Star team, he wasn't eagerly waiting by a phone, repeatedly checking to make sure it was working. He wasn't glued to the TV for the announcement.

Thompson was in the park walking his dog, Rocco.

Another live illustration of Thompson's low-frills ways came during the media circuit.

Curry's entourage included the head of Warriors PR, the manager from his agency representation and the head of Warriors security. Plus a quartet of media followed him around.

Green followed Curry. He had a representative from his agency, the head of Warriors PR, the other half of the Warriors' two-man security team and his personal manager.

Klay Thompson's entourage: the third person on the Warriors' PR totem pole and a freelance security person the team hired.

"And that's why it works," Warriors general manager Bob Myers said. "Maybe Klay is smarter than us all." Don't get it wrong: Thompson has come to like the recognition. But not because it comes with shoe deals and VIP access and fanfare. He likes it mostly because of what it says about his career.

Thompson didn't have nearly as many people at his podium as Curry and Green. But Thompson answered every question with a smile and then went and became a member of the media.

"Klay wants you to pass him the ball every time," Thompson said, speaking in third person while pointing his phone toward Green as if it were a mic. "You're going to do that for him?"

Green responded by pledging to feed Thompson.

"I used to drag my feet on this stuff," Thompson said on his way to another interview. "But I've learned this is all part of it. If you are a great player, this comes with the territory. You've got to embrace it."

Thompson hoists the NBA Western Conference championship trophy with teammate Steph Curry after winning Game 7 against Oklahoma City 96-88.
(Jose Carlos Fajardo/Staff)

# SMILING THROUGH THE PAIN

## Kerr Tries to Keep Medical Struggle from Becoming a Distraction

### By Tim Kawakami | May 5, 2016

Steve Kerr cannot say it's over because it's not over.

Maybe some days and nights are better than others, especially when he's immersed in his job on the sidelines and the Warriors are winning and Oracle Arena is thumping.

Other days are not so good for Kerr, and he admits this, still, more than six months after he started suffering from complications due to spinal cord leakage during back surgery.

He does not talk about it much. He does not want to be the center of attention at any time, and especially when his head hurts almost every waking minute and when he doesn't want his team spending playoff energy worrying about him.

The pain has lessened a bit, and Kerr has felt better and better since his return to the Warriors sidelines in late-January.

But it's not gone, it's not over, and nobody knows when it will be.

"Well, I'd like to say that all that is behind me, but it's really not," Kerr said on the "Warriors Plus Minus" podcast with Marcus Thompson II and me. "I'm still dealing with some pain. Still trying to dig my way out of this completely.

"I've gotten a lot further along. But I'm confident that eventually I'll feel like my old self, pain-free and always happy.

"So this has been incredibly challenging. It's hard to explain to people, so I don't bother. Not that I really want everybody to know what I'm going through, anyway.

Kerr said that the 2015-2016 NBA season was "the hardest year of my life, not even close," yet it culminated in an NBA Coach of the Year award and a second consecutive NBA Finals appearance. (Dan Honda/Staff)

"But I can tell you that it is absolutely changing my perspective on life and on my job and how I approach everything."

The perspective isn't just about coaching, of course, because Kerr's life is hardly just about coaching.

When, at his NBA Coach of the Year news conference, Kerr flatly declared that this was the "hardest year of my life, not even close," that wasn't about basketball at all.

But in this moment, as the Warriors barrel through the second round of the playoffs — up 2-0 on Portland — and are this close to back-to-back championships, I had one specific question for Kerr:

Has this grueling experience perhaps caused you to think you might not want to coach much longer than one or two more years?

The answer came quick and decisively: No, the opposite.

"I imagine I'm going to be coaching for 15 or 20 (years)," Kerr said. "I love — love — what I do. This is my passion. I love being part of a team. I'm incredibly lucky obviously to be coaching a great team right off the bat.

"But we have a chance to make this a long run. I would love nothing more than to be part of this here in Golden State for the next decade."

Coaching isn't what caused the headaches and ringing in his ears. If anything, getting back on the sidelines and smashing clipboards is what helped save Steve Kerr this season.

Even a casual Warriors fan can probably see the signs: Sometimes Kerr squints hard under the arena lights or in front of the camera lenses during games or news conferences.

But his good friend and assistant coach Bruce Fraser said Kerr has always been sharp mentally through his comeback, and that once he returned, he was fiercely determined to do the job as he always has.

Steve Kerr, left, and majority owner Joe Lacob talk in the hallway before the start of a Warriors game against the Los Angeles Lakers at Oracle. Lacob and team management were very supportive of Kerr during his health struggles. (Doug Duran/Staff)

# "I imagine I'm going to be coaching for 15 or 20 (years). I love — love — what I do. This is my passion. I love being part of a team. I'm incredibly lucky obviously to be coaching a great team right off the bat."
## —Steve Kerr

"I've always known he was tough and a fighter," Fraser said, "but he's really fought without people seeing it."

Fraser said Kerr never announces if this particular day is a good or bad one, but Fraser can tell by sensing Kerr's energy level.

Game 1 vs. Portland, for instance, was a great energy day for Kerr, as Fraser noted to assistant Luke Walton at the time.

When Fraser has guessed that Kerr's energy is low, Fraser has at times prodded Walton to get more vocal with the players — the way Walton stepped in for Kerr during the first 43 games of this season.

The Warriors front office wholly understood this from the beginning of Kerr's ordeal. His recovery had no set timetable and Kerr would return when he felt he could.

Kerr got back to coaching not because he was fully healthy, but because it was better to be doing something he loved while feeling terrible than to be doing nothing at home and feeling worse.

"It's easy to see why people thought, 'He's back at work, everything's great,'" general manager Bob Myers said. "That would be the natural assumption.

"But it was more of, 'Look, I'm not feeling good sitting at home watching the team on the road, sitting in the back, watching from the locker room or from the coach's office.

"So let's get back at it and as long as I don't get worse I'm going to do it that way.'"

Kerr suggested he really knew he was back into some kind of coaching groove when he smashed a clipboard during the team's victory in New York on Jan. 31 — his fifth game back.

Still, Kerr said his health struggle has given him a new perspective, a broader view of things beyond coaching and a richer view of coaching itself.

"I'm still as competitive as ever," Kerr said. "But the games aren't the end-all, be-all. As much as I want to win, I have truly been given the perspective that health is the only thing that really matters. Your own health, the health of your family and friends.

"It sounds like a cliché, but when you go through something like this you truly feel it."

These days, sometimes Kerr sounds more like a Zen guru than Gregg Popovich's peer, but there's a practical point to this.

His theme: Find joy when you can, because you don't know if what you have will go away, or if you'll get sick, or if you get a headache that never goes away.

Kerr has connected that to his life, to the Warriors' playoff situation and to everything.

Kerr has lived through great things and terrible things in his life, and nothing was more terrible than the murder of his father Malcolm Kerr, president of American University in Beirut, in 1984.

"He's had a pretty charmed life, relatively," Fraser said. "He's had amazing things happen to him through his intellect and his work ethic.

"But his dad passing away was a really tough thing for him. Really tough. He channeled that into a positive, where he was able to focus ... small things didn't matter any more.

"That was a life-changing event for him. I would say this was another one."

Maybe this is what drove Kerr to tell Fraser on Christmas Eve that he was ready to start coaching for the Christmas game against Cleveland.

It was too soon, but he wanted back so bad.

Recently, Kerr admitted that there were times during his leave of absence that he wondered if he'd make it back.

But those who know him best knew he was coming back because he loved coaching too much to consider anything else.

He's back. He's still miserable sometimes. But miserable and coaching beats the alternative by so much that Kerr doesn't even need to spell it out. 🏀

Steve Kerr missed the first 43 games of the 2015-2016 season with back issues but with the help of interim coach Luke Walton, helped lead the Warriors to an NBA record 73 wins. (Jose Carlos Fajardo/Staff)

# PROVEN

## How a Ticked-Off Draymond Green Fell into the Warriors' Lap

### By Jon Wilner | May 20, 2016

The topic is the 2012 NBA draft — this draft — and Warriors forward Draymond Green has his game face on. Offered a printout of every selection to assist his recollections of that fateful night, Green scoffs.

"I don't need it."

And with that, he begins.

"First was Anthony Davis to New Orleans," he says. "Then Charlotte took (Michael) Kidd-Gilchrist. Then Washington took Bradley Beal. Fourth was Cleveland: Dion Waiters.

"Eight was Toronto: Terrence Ross ...

"Sixteen was Houston: Royce White ...

By the time he's done, Green has reeled off the names of all 34 players selected ahead of him and the corresponding team.

In order.

Ticked off? You're darn right he's still ticked off.

"I know why I had to wait," he said. "I know what the scouts thought: 'He's a tweener. Who's he going to guard? He's maxed out his potential.'

"But I knew none of that was valid. What happened to me is what normally happens to players in my situation. But I knew I wasn't normal."

Four years after he was labeled too small for power forward and not skilled enough for the wing, Green is one of the NBA's dominant forces. The indomitable heart of the team that won a league-record 73 games, he finished seventh in the MVP race, was second in defensive player of the year voting and has redefined the power forward position.

Draymond Green's versatility will be invaluable when integrating Kevin Durant into the offense and spreading the ball around among the Warriors' plethora of weapons. (Jane Tyska/Staff)

# The Warriors not only passed on Green once but twice — with the No. 7 and No. 30 selections — before grabbing him with the fifth pick of the second round (35th overall).

In any redraft of the 2012 prospects, Green would be no worse than the third selection behind New Orleans' Davis and Portland's Damian Lillard.

"I'm surprised by the level he's achieved so quickly," said Warriors personnel director Larry Harris, who scouted Green extensively during his career at Michigan State. "But I'm not surprised he got there."

The Warriors not only passed on Green once but twice — with the No. 7 and No. 30 selections — before grabbing him with the fifth pick of the second round (35th overall).

"We kind of blew it," general manager Bob Myers said with a laugh. "But at least we got him."

Despite his long memory and the boulder on his shoulder, Green doesn't tease Myers about passing on him.

"It's hard to give them (bleep) about it," he said, "because what they did makes perfect sense."

The tale, like the list of players picked ahead of Green, is worth recounting.

## Setting the Table

The process that led to Green joining the Warriors began, as so many Warriors processes once began, with a thud.

On Feb. 23, 2011, then-general manager Larry Riley shipped center Dan Gadzuric and forward Brandan Wright to the New Jersey (now Brooklyn) Nets in exchange for forward Troy Murphy, by then in the final stages of his career, and a second-round pick in the 2012 draft.

The trade was received poorly by Warriors fans, who had hoped a bevy of expiring contracts would prove valuable in the midseason trade market. But it was not to be. Within a week, Murphy was waived. The second-round pick in 2012? It seemed like a bone tossed to a junkyard dog.

But Riley believed otherwise. The Warriors had assessed New Jersey's roster and calculated that a below-average season could be in the works for the Nets in 2011-12. They also examined the list of college players likely to be eligible for the '12 draft and concluded there might be more first-round prospects than first-round slots.

"We wanted to eliminate the players who wouldn't be a factor for us," Riley said of the trade. "The likelihood of attracting a good free agent to Golden State wasn't real high, but it's not unusual for a second-round pick to become a pretty good player.

"From (picks) 45 through 60, it's tough. But we placed value on second rounders, especially the first 15 picks of the second round."

Two weeks later after the trade, Green played one of the finest all-around games of his college career, leading Michigan State to a Big Ten tournament victory with a stat line that would become familiar to Warriors fans: 21 points, 14 rebounds, four assists, two steals and two blocked shots.

Although a bit overweight, Green, a junior, had emerged as an intriguing NBA prospect. The Warriors began their due diligence.

"We checked into Draymond's family, who he hung around with at school, who he stayed in touch with from high school," Harris said. "There were no issues. Everything came back the same: He was very intense, and he hated to lose at anything. That's carried over, obviously."

Green high-fives fans after a 108-97 win against the Cleveland Cavaliers in Game 4 of the 2016 NBA Finals. (Nhat V. Meyer/Staff)

The Warriors were not alone in their appreciation for Green's skills and smarts — or in wondering where he would fit in the pros. Could he defend bigger power forwards? Would he force defenses to play him honestly on the perimeter? "He wasn't totally broken as a shooter," Riley said.

In NBA parlance, Green was a classic tweener.

The pivot point for Riley came in February of Green's senior season, when he attended a Michigan State-Ohio State showdown on a snowy Sunday afternoon.

"It was so cold, and I was struggling to get myself into the game," Riley recalled. "But Draymond played his tail off" — 12 points, nine rebounds — "and I remember walking out of the arena thinking, 'There's something about this guy. Somehow, he's going to make it at the next level.'"

Possibly for the Warriors.

"At the time," Riley added, "we needed players with big hearts."

# Ready to Celebrate

On draft night, approximately 100 of Green's friends and family members filed into the Dow Events Center in Saginaw, Michigan, his hometown, for a celebration. Most projections had Green going in the final 10 picks of the first round, but there were warning signs.

Atlanta had expressed strong interest, but three days before the draft, the Hawks announced general manager Rick Sund's contract would not be extended.

Larry Bird, Indiana's president of basketball operations, was intrigued enough to invite Green for two workouts at the Pacers' facility. But the day before the draft, Larry Legend stepped down as part of an executive reorganization by the Pacers.

Memphis had given Green the impression it was interested. Same with the Warriors, who rated Green "in the low 20s" on their master list of prospects, according to Myers. Not surprisingly, he wasn't part of the discussion for the No. 7 pick, which was used to draft North Carolina forward Harrison Barnes.

As the first round unfolded, the anxiety level rose in the Dow Events Center in Saginaw.

At No. 23, Atlanta passed on Green to select guard John Jenkins.

At No. 26, Indiana passed on Green to pick center Miles Plumlee.

"That's when we started to get nervous," said Michigan State assistant coach Dwayne Stephens, who attended the party and remains a close friend.

More big men were scooped up, then a guard. Finally, the Warriors were back on the clock with the 30th and final pick of the first round — a pick they had obtained from San Antonio a few months earlier in the Stephen Jackson trade.

Nerves were frayed in Saginaw, but spirits were high in the Warriors' draft room: They had two good options.

"We were shocked (Green) was there," Myers said.

The 2015-2016 NBA season saw Green become a true superstar, averaging 14 points, 9.5 rebounds, and 7.4 assists. He also garnered his first All-Star selection and second NBA All-Defensive First-Team honor. (Nhat V. Meyer/Staff)

But they were also fond of Festus Ezeli, a big man from Vanderbilt who offered something Green could not: Six feet and 11 inches of rim protection.

"We had a long discussion about which way to go," Harris said. "We're thinking: What's the sound decision and what are the ramifications?

"It's so hard to get size. Our intel told us that if we picked Draymond, Festus wouldn't last (until the 35th pick). But there was a chance Draymond would still be there."

Ezeli was the pick.

# Night to Remember

At the Dow Events Center, a heartbroken Green retreated to a backroom, consoled by his mother and several close friends.

He knew the teams at the top of the second round (Charlotte, Washington and Dallas, which had two picks) were unlikely to call his name. If the Warriors passed on him at 35, Green set his sights on Detroit with the 39th pick. General manager Joe Dumars had been a father-figure to Green over the years.

"I told my agent that if it wasn't Golden State, he should tell the next three teams that I was going to play overseas, so Detroit could take me," Green said.

The first player off the board in the second round, to Charlotte, was small forward Jeffery Taylor.

In their draft room, the Warriors hoped a foreign player would shorten the bridge to Green. Sure enough, Washington took Tomas Satoransky, a guard from the Czech Republic,

with the 32nd pick. Two spots separated the Warriors from Green, and both belonged to Dallas.

Harris' intel proved to be spot on: So desperate for size were the Mavericks that they used the 33rd pick on a 6-foot-10 project named Bernard James, who was 27 years old and had served in the military before attending college.

At No. 34, the Mavericks took Jae Crowder, a small forward from Marquette.

The Warriors celebrated. Their gamble had paid off: Green was on the board.

"He was the guy," Myers said. "There was no debate."

In Saginaw, there was only relief. Green took a little time before returning to the party with a smile on his face.

"He needed to digest it all," Stephens said. "It put a chip on his shoulder."

The experience is seared into Green's memory. Not only can he recite the name of each player selected ahead of him, in order, he knows their whereabouts.

He knows, for example, that John Jenkins, selected by Atlanta in the spot Green thought was his, has been injured, waived and assigned multiple times to the D-League.

He knows Plumlee, selected by the Pacers, is a journeyman on his third team in four years.

He knows Taylor, the first pick of the second round, is playing in Spain.

"I will never forget that night," he said. "I had to wait all that time. I'm not saying I'm cocky or anything, but I felt like I had to wait behind guys I was better than.

"And I think I've proven it."

Draymond Green and majority owner Joe Lacob pose with the NBA championship trophy after the Warriors' 105-97 win over the Cleveland Cavaliers in Game 6 of the 2015 NBA Finals. (Nhat V. Meyer/Staff)

# RING IN THE NEW YEAR

## Durant and the Warriors Primed for a Championship Run

By Anthony Slater | September 29, 2016

The last game the Seattle SuperSonics ever played was at Oracle Arena. They won. The Warriors were solid that season: 48-34. But that night, Golden State was shredded by a string-bean teenager.

It was April 16, 2008. Kevin Durant was 19 years old. He made 18 of his 25 shots, finishing with 42 points, 13 rebounds and six assists. A few weeks later, he was named Rookie of the Year.

"What a show he put on," then-Warriors coach Don Nelson said. "Wow. I knew he was good, but he's going to be a superstar."

It was Golden State's first real brush with Durant's greatness. Over the next eight years, they'd be victimized by it again and again. But no more. Now they'll be the beneficiary. As Durant enters the prime years of his path to the Hall of Fame, he's a Warrior.

He could have been a Blazer.

Greg Oden versus Kevin Durant. That was the debate back in 2007. KD was the shy shooter from the University of Texas. He had guard skills, a pure stroke, a center's height but a slender frame. Oden was Goliath, a throwback big man who could bang and board and dunk and patrol the paint. Portland went with bulk over skill. Bulk broke down. Skill rose up.

Durant's biggest pre-draft knock was his weight room numbers. At the combine, he failed to bench-press 185 pounds. It became the crux of the argument against taking him, a confirmation that the skinny dude couldn't thrive in a physical league. Forget the 26 points and 11 rebounds he averaged as a freshman at Texas. The rhetoric went wild.

"He's a wing that can't bench 185," radio host Colin Cowherd ranted. "Danica Patrick

Kevin Durant dunks as Toronto Raptors' Patrick Paterson looks on. It will be a familiar site as the Warriors consistently push the ball in transition this season. (AP Images)

# "You have to train your mind to know this is important for you, this is gonna help you long term. You just gotta stay disciplined."
# —Kevin Durant

can bench 185. So can Dan Patrick. That's embarrassing."

Durant hushed critics quickly with that massive rookie year. But his frail frame was still a roadblock — the difference between an All-Star and a legend. The NBA schedule was grueling. Defenders were grown men. They still couldn't reach his unblockable shot, but they were sturdier and smarter. And they had a scouting report: Bruise him up, push him around.

Growing up in Washington D.C., Durant was around weight rooms but never in them. The machines were too cramped, the exercises too awkward for his lanky frame. Plus his success made it seem like a waste of time. Why lift like that guy when I just put 30 points on that guy?

"I need to go in there when I'm already playing well?" he remembered questioning. "I'm already growing as a player with this size and frame."

But the NBA highlighted the importance of adding strength. As the Sonics turned into the Thunder and KD moved from Seattle to Oklahoma City, the organization created a growth plan. It had to be gradual. They couldn't just pump out Hulk KD in one off-season. That could be detrimental. They needed him to put on muscle carefully, so as not to disrupt the extreme skill.

Durant was 212 pounds as a rookie in 2007, then 223 by 2009, 231 by 2011, 237 by 2013 and around 242 last season. He improved his diet, reducing the fast-food trips and loading up on protein, mostly from salmon, sea bass and steak from grass-fed cattle. But a commitment to the weight room was key.

"You have to train your mind to know this is important for you, this is gonna help you long term," he said. "You just gotta stay disciplined."

Durant's game exploded. At 21, he became the youngest scoring champ ever, averaging 30.1 points his third year. That season, he started a streak of seven straight All-Star appearances, which is ongoing.

Durant would win three more scoring titles over the next four seasons, giving him four before his 26th birthday. In NBA history, only Michael Jordan (10) and Wilt Chamberlain (7) have more.

The rest of Durant's game rounded out, too. He quickly morphed into a top-25 rebounder, a 1-per night shot-blocker and a reliable playmaker. Durant averaged 2.4 assists as a rookie. He averaged 5.5 in his seventh season, the year he won MVP.

As his game matured, so did Durant's mind and personality. He entered the league shy and reserved. Playing in

An NBA championship is all that's missing from Kevin Durant's illustrious career and this Warriors team gives him a great opportunity to change that. (AP Images)

middle America, he was viewed as game's wholesome superstar. He'd show up at press conferences in those early years with a backpack, as if the school bell had just rung. In the backpack were his Bible and his iPod.

At 23, back in 2012, KD and his young Thunder shockingly ascended to the NBA Finals. There, they fell to LeBron James and the Heat. Post series, hot-take criticisms arose. Durant didn't have the killer instinct, they said.

So Nike pushed back against that talk, releasing a new marketing campaign in early 2013: KD Is Not Nice.

On the court, Durant was less nice. His first four seasons, he had seven technical fouls, total. Over the next three seasons, he was hit for 33.

Off the court, his likable persona shone through. In 2013, his charity donated $1 million to the Red Cross for tornado relief after a wicked twister rocked Oklahoma. In 2014, he delivered his famous MVP speech, singling out each teammate and then, through tears, telling his mother: "You the real MVP."

But the inability to get over the hump seemed to eat at him. Once the league's darling, the Thunder turned into a snake-bitten punching bag, losing key guys to injuries at inopportune times. There was massive success, including four conference finals appearances in six years.

But no titles meant no mercy from pundits. They roasted Kendrick Perkins, one of Durant's best friends, and questioned Russell Westbrook, the point guard he publicly backed. KD seethed. He got edgier in interviews. He bit back at the media, at one point telling reporters: "Y'all don't know (bleep)."

He was most ornery during the 2014-15 season. Durant had three surgeries on his right foot that year, missing 55 games. Frustration bled from his interviews. Another season passed without a coveted title. This time he watched helplessly in a walking boot.

But KD returned the next year — last season — refreshed. He had a new coach, Billy Donovan, a repaired foot and an impending free agency that loomed over it all. Distractions were everywhere. But his game remained uniquely potent. Durant put up monster regular season numbers again and then helped slay the 67-win Spurs in the second round.

The Thunder then went up 3-1 on the 73-win Warriors in the West Finals. Led by Durant, OKC finally looked ready to win it all.

But the dream crumbled again, this time in hideous fashion. The Thunder lost three straight games to Golden State and then, a month later, Durant stunned the sports world by joining the Warriors.

On the court, Durant has done just about everything in his nine seasons. But at 28, he's still without a ring. That's why he is here. 🏀

The addition of Kevin Durant gives the Warriors a collection of scorers unlike anything ever seen in the NBA. (Jane Tyska/Staff)